THE EXCHEQUER
IN THE
TWELFTH CENTURY

THE FORD LECTURES
DELIVERED IN THE UNIVERSITY OF OXFORD
IN MICHAELMAS TERM, 1911

By REGINALD L. POOLE, M.A., LL.D.
KEEPER OF THE ARCHIVES
AND FELLOW OF MAGDALEN COLLEGE

THE LAWBOOK EXCHANGE, LTD.
Clark, New Jersey
2006

ISBN-13: 978-1-58477-658-1
ISBN-10: 1-58477-658-7

Printed in the United States of America on acid-free paper

THE LAWBOOK EXCHANGE, LTD.
33 Terminal Avenue
Clark, New Jersey 07066-1321

Please see our website for a selection of our other publications and fine facsimile reprints of classic works of legal history:
www.lawbookexchange.com

Library of Congress Cataloging-in-Publication Data

Poole, Reginald Lane, 1857-1939.
The Exchequer in the twelfth century / Reginald Lane Poole.
p. cm.
Originally published: Oxford : Clarendon press, 1912.
Includes bibliographical references and index.
ISBN 1-58477-658-7 (alk. paper)
1. Great Britain. Exchequer. 2. Finance--Great Britain--History. I. Title.

HJ1030.P66 2005
336.42'09'021--dc22 2005000906

THE EXCHEQUER
IN THE
TWELFTH CENTURY

THE FORD LECTURES
DELIVERED IN THE UNIVERSITY OF OXFORD
IN MICHAELMAS TERM, 1911

BY REGINALD L. POOLE, M.A., LL.D.
KEEPER OF THE ARCHIVES
AND FELLOW OF MAGDALEN COLLEGE

OXFORD
AT THE CLARENDON PRESS
1912

PREFACE

TEN years ago I gave a course of lectures on the Dialogus de Scaccario, and the book interested me so much that I determined to remodel my materials so as to form a treatise on the subject. My preparations, however, went on slowly, and it was not until I retired from College work in the summer of 1910 that I had leisure to advance them very much. My election as Ford's Lecturer in English History, in November of that year, gave me the opportunity of planning in a different form the book which I had contemplated. The form was necessarily that of a course of lectures; but the subject was not the Dialogue but the Exchequer itself. I have printed the lectures substantially as they were delivered in last October and November; but I have enlarged the introduction to the first lecture into a separate chapter, and I have added a supplementary lecture, which, though prepared, there was not time to deliver. Hence the six lectures now appear as eight chapters.

The form of a lecture will explain and partly excuse the limitations and defects of the work. In a lecture a certain amount of repetition is unavoidable: it is necessary also to avoid obscurity of statement; one must not introduce reserves and qualifications overmuch. I have no doubt that I have made many rash assertions and not a few technical mistakes. But I have sought before all things to be plain and free from ambiguity in expression. It has also resulted that a great deal of illustrative detail has been omitted. Part of this has indeed been supplied by means of notes. But a large area has been designedly left untouched. I have considered the Exchequer as a machine at work and have tried to explain how it worked. This was all that I could attempt within the limitations of a short course. The other side of the subject, the sources from which the payments came, I have treated summarily. To have entered at all usefully into such matters as the assessment of Danegeld or of scutage would have required an apparatus of detailed calculations which could not practically have been given in lecture; and it would besides have distracted attention from my main subject.

Confining myself in principle to the twelfth century, while I have briefly indicated the continuity of various offices down to modern times, I have avoided saying anything of the more complicated system of controlling the business of the Exchequer which arose when the practice of enrolling the Chancery records led to the making of estreats and counterwrits, or of the specialization of accounts which began under Edward I.

Nor have I entered upon the wide field occupied by the remembrancers in subsequent times, though I have given reason for believing that their offices were already in existence. Until the memoranda rolls are accessible in print it will hardly be possible to survey with profit the work which fell to the remembrancers' departments.

It will prevent misunderstanding if I mention that in my frequent quotations from the Dialogue I never profess to give a strict translation. I render freely and usually abridge. My obligations to the editors of the Oxford edition of that work are, I hope, sufficiently implied in what I have said of it in my opening chapter, which also explains the nature of my indebtedness to other writers. But I should like to thank Messrs. C. G. Crump, Charles Johnson, and C. Hilary Jenkinson, of the Public Record Office, for their extreme kindness in answering questions which I addressed to them at various times. Had I ventured to ask any of them to look over my proof sheets, I am sure the text would have been freed from many errors. Nor should I omit to express my gratitude to the Secretary to the Delegates of the Clarendon Press for the readiness with which he arranged for my convenience that my lectures should all be in print before they were delivered.

R. L. P.

January 1912.

CONTENTS

I

TEXTS AND COMMENTARIES

THE wealth of England in records for the earlier middle ages—I speak of the time before the thirteenth century—is unapproached by any other country in Europe. It is not in our historians that we claim a pre-eminence, though it was monks from the British Isles who traced the models upon which all the compilations of Frankish Annals were founded. But no other country possesses anything like the mass of land charters such as we have for the Anglo-Saxon period. No other country has a survey such as that of our Domesday Book. Abroad there are a few customals of particular lordships, such as the invaluable polyptych of Irmino; but for a survey on a great scale we have to wait until the beginning of the fourteenth century, when the *Urbar* or terrier of the Habsburg lands was drawn up. In England almost the whole country was minutely surveyed before William the Conqueror had finished his reign. The Domesday survey, like a modern valuation return, was compiled as a basis for taxation; and it is in the revenue department that our earliest official records appear. The great annual rolls of the Exchequer are nearly complete for the reign of

Henry II and the time following, and one single specimen is preserved from the reign of Henry I. Here again there is no parallel abroad except under the same dynasty in Normandy, where however the rolls now preserved do not begin until 1180.

Our series of rolls, generally known by their later name of Pipe Rolls, were the subject of minute study by the learned and indefatigable Thomas Madox, whose History and Antiquities of the Exchequer, published in 1711,[1] is never likely to be superseded in these days of rapid and perfunctory work. But the texts themselves remained unpublished until, thanks to the Record Commission, Joseph Hunter printed the four oldest rolls in 1833 and 1844, and one of the first year of Richard I also in 1844. More recently a private society was established for the purpose of continuing the publication, and since 1884 (with an interval between 1900 and 1904) this Pipe Roll Society has issued 31 volumes, all but six of which are devoted to the particular rolls from which it takes its name. The fact that all these new materials are now placed at our disposal is an incentive to make the attempt to take a general survey of the institution from which they proceed; but it

[1] My references are to the pages of this edition, but I have cited also the chapter and section for the convenience of those who use the edition of 1769. An italic letter following the page indicates a footnote.

should be said at the outset that a comparison of successive rolls, however valuable for the purpose of discovering and ascertaining the succession to lands and offices, does not serve substantially to modify the conclusions as to the working of the exchequer system which might be drawn from the study of a couple of rolls.

Nor must it be supposed that the pipe rolls profess to contain anything like a complete record of the business which was transacted at the Exchequer. In order to learn this we have to take recourse to a work which is yet another instance of the extraordinary abundance of our historical materials and which is the envy of continental students. The famous Dialogue concerning the Exchequer was not merely written by one who was himself treasurer, but it is written with such fullness and lucidity of statement as to leave very few matters, and those not of the first importance, in obscurity. The author, Richard bishop of London, set out to explain the system in which he had been trained, and he succeeded to a degree which we can hardly overpraise. That I may not seem to exaggerate the merits of a work which must necessarily be one of my leading authorities, I will quote some sentences from Maitland, whose judgement, here at any rate, will not be disparaged.

[1] The book stands out as an unique book in the history of medieval England, perhaps in the history of medieval

[1] History of English Law, 1895, i. 140 f.

Europe. A high officer of state, the trusted counsellor of a powerful king, undertakes to explain to all whom it may concern the machinery of government. He will not deal in generalities, he will condescend to minute details. Perhaps his book was not meant for the general public so much as for the numerous clerks who were learning their business in the exchequer, but still that such a book should be written, is one of the wonderful things of Henry's wonderful reign. We may safely say that it was not published without the king's licence, and yet it exposes to the light of day many things which kings and ministers are apt to treat as solemn mysteries of state. We should know far more of the history of government than will ever be known could we have a Dialogue on the Exchequer from every century; but we have one only and it comes from the reign of Henry II. Henry was so strong that he had nothing to conceal; he could stand criticism; his will and pleasure if properly explained to his subjects would appear as reasonable and at any rate would not be resisted. And so his treasurer expounded the course of proceedings in the exchequer, the constitution of this financial board, its writs and its rolls, the various sources of royal income, the danegeld and the murder fine, the collection of the debts due to the king, the treatment of his debtors, and, coming to details, he described the chessboard and the counters, the tallies, the scales, and the melting pot. But for him, we should have known little of the administrative and fiscal law of his time or of later times—for the rolls of the exchequer sadly need a commentary—but as it is, we may know much.

The authorship of the Dialogue is not now disputed, but it was long obscured by several confusions. Bishop Bale copied from the collections of Nicholas Brigham an extract from the book relative to the author's lost work, the Tricolumnis, and afterwards wrote, apparently as a guess, the name of Gervase of Tilbury between the lines of his manuscript.[1] The conjecture was repeated as a fact in his published Catalogue of British Writers,[2] and was long accepted. But, as Madox pointed out, Gervase the marshal of Burgundy under the Emperor Otto IV was unquestionably a layman, and the author of the Dialogue was as certainly a clergyman.[3] Gervase also wrote about twenty years later than the time when the Dialogue was composed. Another cause of confusion was that the Dialogue was often read in late copies of the Red Book or the Black Book of the Exchequer, and hence passages from the Dialogue are quoted as from the Red or Black Book.[4] Possibly one copy of this book belonged to Nicholas Ockham in the time of Edward I and chanced to have his

[1] Index Britanniae Scriptorum, Oxford, 1902, p. 477.

[2] Scriptorum illustrium maioris Brytannię Catalogus, Basel 1557, iii. 58 p. 250.

[3] See the Dissertatio epistolaris addressed to lord Halifax, prefixed to his edition of the Dialogus at the end of his History of the Exchequer, pp. x, xi. The author of the Dialogue expressly describes himself as a clergyman, ii. 26 p. 245.

[4] Selden cites it from *libro Rub. Archiu. Scacc.*: Titles of Honor, ii. 5, 2nd ed. 1631, p. 687. Prynne, in his Aurum Reginae, 1668, p. 4, says that it was 'stiled by most, *The Red Book of the Exchequer*'. Sir Matthew Hale, in his Short Treatise touching Sheriffs Accompts, 1683, p. 21, refers to 'Gervasius Tilburiensis, or the black Book of the Exchequer, written in the time of H. 2'.

name written upon it; anyhow lord chief justice Coke refers to the Dialogue as by Ockham:[1] it is not necessary to suppose that he was thinking of the famous schoolman.[2] Madox at last settled the true authorship, which had, as he pointed out,[3] been in fact clearly stated by Alexander Swerford, the editor of the Red Book of the Exchequer in the second quarter of the thirteenth century.[4]

Richard the Treasurer belonged to the most characteristic official family of his time.[5] His

---

[1] 'Ockam who wrote in the raigne of Henry the second:' Coke upon Littleton (First Institute), 1628, p. 13.

[2] Sir Henry Spelman in his Glossarium archaiologicum (3rd ed., 1687), cites the Dialogue under the name of Niger liber fiscalis (pp. 202 *a*, 331 *a*), Niger liber Scaccarii (p. 229 *b*) and *Ockamus qui sub excessu Edouardi 2 floruit* (p. 331 *b*), as well as under that of Gervase of Tilbury (p. 502 *a*). Compare the Athenaeum, no. 3933 p. 331 *b*, 14 March 1903.

[3] Dissertatio epistolaris, pp. xi, xii. In the preface to his Firma Burgi, 1726, § 10, Madox mentions that Selden learned from Agard on the authority of Swerford that the Dialogue was written 'by Richard Bishop of London (his name being Richard de Beaumes) under Henrie I'; so, even when Swerford's words were vouched in evidence, they were not correctly understood.

[4] 'Ricardus Londoniensis episcopus, licet in sui libelli tractatu superius multa de negotiis scaccarii digererit:' Red Book of the Exchequer, p. 4 (where the edition has *degererit*). This is on fo. 47 of the manuscript; *superius* refers back to the Dialogue, which ends on fo. 46.

[5] See the admirable account of his life in Professor Felix Liebermann's Einleitung in den Dialogus de Scaccario, Göttingen 1875, which has served as the basis of all that has been written since on the subject.

great-uncle Roger bishop of Salisbury, a Norman from Caen,[1] was chancellor and then justiciar under Henry I. As justiciar, for long periods he held the reins of the government of the country,[2] and it was under him that the Exchequer was instituted. His nephew, Nigel or Neal, was employed in the business of the king's Court as early as 1126 or 1127,[3] and in 1133 was made bishop of Ely. When Stephen became king, Roger remained justiciar, his son Richard was chancellor, and his nephew treasurer. In 1139 the family suffered an eclipse, and Roger died the same year. Neal recovered his bishopric in 1141, but though actively engaged as a baron of the Exchequer, he was never again treasurer.[4] His son Richard, with whom we are more directly concerned, was born in 1130 or perhaps a little earlier, before his father was in priest's orders, and was brought up in the monastery of Ely. It is not known when he entered the king's service; it has been thought that he was keeper of the seal:[5] but, apparently in 1158, bishop Neal bought the treasurership for him

---

[1] William of Newburgh i. 6, in Chronicles of Stephen, Henry II, and Richard I, ed. R. Howlett, i (1884) 36.

[2] William of Malmesbury, Gesta Regum, § 408, ed. Stubbs, 1889, ii. 483 f.

[3] See below, p. 57.

[4] Madox, p. 141, inclined to think that he was; but the evidence he quotes only calls him baron, p. 142 *b*. See Liebermann, p. 24 note 4 and p. 33.

[5] The *clericus qui praeest scriptorio*: see Liebermann, p. 33 n. 2. On this officer see below, pp. 110 f.

for £400.[1] Meanwhile he advanced in ecclesiastical preferments. By 1169 he was archdeacon of Ely, ten years later canon of St. Paul's, in 1184 dean of Lincoln. Finally in 1189 he was made bishop of London, and held the see with the treasurership until his death in 1198.[2]

The Dialogue was written before he was dean or bishop. The first book opens with the words, 'In the twenty-third year of the reign of king Henry II, while I sat at the window of the tower which is by the river Thames,'[3] on the east side of Westminster Hall. This gives the year ending, according to the Exchequer rule, at Michaelmas 1177. But later on[4] the author mentions a provision made by the king at Michaelmas 1178, so that either the composition of the work was not finished until after that date or else the passage is a later insertion. In any case the work was completed before the spring of 1179, for it mentions the division of England for judicial purposes into six circuits, and

---

1 Richard of Ely, Historia Eliensis, in H. Wharton's Anglia sacra, i. 627, 1691. I follow Dr. Liebermann for the date. R. W. Eyton, in his Court, Household, and Itinerary of Henry II, 1878, p. 341, says '1159', but gives no reference.

2 The *secretum* of bishop Richard appears as a counterseal on a charter granted by him to the monks of Bec which is preserved among the muniments of the dean and canons of St. George's chapel, Windsor (XI. G. 7). The legend is PAVLVS SERVVS CRISTI IHS.

3 i. 1 p. 170.

4 i. 8 p. 200.

before Whitsuntide[1] in that year the king altered the number to four.[2]

Bishop Richard I believe to be a writer whose statements may be accepted as absolutely trustworthy so far as his knowledge and experience of the working of the Exchequer carry him. When he tries to explain the origin and cause of many of its practices he quite excusably goes wrong. A good deal of ridicule has been poured upon him for errors of this sort, and it has often been left to be implied that he is almost equally open to suspicion in regard to what he says of the system of his own day. But the two things are quite independent. I doubt whether every modern chancellor of the Exchequer could give you an intelligible account of the way in which a most important official, the comptroller[3] and auditor-general, came to perform two functions which are not necessarily, nor indeed naturally, connected. As comptroller-general of the Exchequer he or his representative keeps the banking account of the Treasury and signs the cheques: as auditor-general of public accounts he disallows any payment not authorized by parliament. In the one capacity he descends

---

[1] Eyton says on 10 April: p. 226.

[2] Gesta Regis Henrici II, ed. Stubbs, 1867, i. 238 f., cf. 240. See Liebermann, p. 10.

[3] This official spelling embodies an old error, the word being supposed to be connected with *accompt*. The controller is really the *contrarotulator*, one who keeps a counter-roll.

from the old auditor of the Receipt of the Exchequer; in the other, he takes over the duties of the commissioners of public accounts, who represent several offices of audit which can be traced back to early times. The union of the two offices was not completed until 1867; but I believe that many persons well acquainted with public affairs take for granted that a post of such high responsibility, whose powers excite the admiration of foreign observers, must be an ancient element in the constitution, though its most important functions were in fact first created in 1780.[1] In like manner the author of the Dialogue relates the traditions current in the Exchequer, some of which are not only unsupported but are contradicted by known facts. But his mistakes as to the past do not in the least affect the truth and accuracy of his description of what he saw actually in practice in his own time; and the more closely we examine his treatise the more reason we shall find to place confidence in his statements.

The Dialogue was first published in 1711 by Thomas Madox as an appendix to his History and

[1] The commissioners for examining, taking, and stating the public accounts were appointed by the statute of 20 George III c. 54, which was continued and sometimes amended annually until 1785, when by the statute of 25 George III c. 52, they took over the duties of the auditors of the imprest, whose offices were thereby abolished, and were constituted commissioners for auditing the public accounts.

Antiquities of the Exchequer; and his edition professes to be taken from two Exchequer compilations of the thirteenth century known as the Black and the Red Books. But in the Dissertatio epistolaris to lord Halifax, which is prefixed to the edition, Madox explains that he began by causing a transcript to be made of two more recent copies in lord Somers's library. This transcript, with the help of George Holmes, the deputy-keeper of the records in the Tower, he himself collated with the Black and Red Books; and the result is that what we have is a conflate text based upon two late copies but adapted, as far as could be done, to the earlier text of the Black Book,[1] while the earliest text of all, that of the Red Book, was only used for the purpose of emendation and for supplying the titles of the chapters which were absent from the Black Book. Madox's text was reprinted in 1870, with some corrections, by bishop Stubbs in his Select Charters and other Illustrations of

---

[1] The calendar in the Black Book has been assigned to 1239 or 1250 on the ground that Easter Day is entered in it on 27 March: see the Catalogue of Manuscripts and other Objects in the Museum of the Public Record Office, 6th ed., 1909, p. 19. But no argument can be drawn from this. It was the conventional date on which Easter was inserted in calendars, especially in Gaul: see E. A. Loew, Die ältesten Kalendarien aus Monte Cassino, Munich 1908, p. 73. The text of the Dialogus is believed to be in a different hand from the calendar, and was probably written not long before the middle of the thirteenth century.

English Constitutional History, and I shall cite the treatise by the pages of this edition because it is in every one's hand.[1] But a notable advance in the critical treatment of the text was made by Messrs. A. Hughes, C. G. Crump, and C. Johnson, of the Public Record Office, who brought out a new edition of the Dialogue at Oxford in 1902.[2] They produced their text strictly from three manuscripts of the thirteenth century, the two Exchequer books already mentioned and the Cottonian manuscript, Cleopatra A. 16, in the British Museum, which they have fully collated.[3] Though the number of important new readings which they have incorporated is not in fact very large, they have performed the very real service of placing before us the means of judging what the manuscript evidence is, and they have supplied an apparatus of extremely valuable notes. It is however to be regretted that the form in which the edition is printed is one that makes reference to it difficult. The beginnings of the chapters are not clearly marked, and the titles, which are probably almost all original,[4] are omitted. Still,

[1] I use the fifth edition, 1884, the pages of which agree with those of the eighth edition, 1900.

[2] De necessariis Observantiis Scaccarii Dialogus, commonly called Dialogus de Scaccario, by Richard, son of Nigel, Treasurer of England and Bishop of London.

[3] As far as book ii. 18: the rest is a fifteenth-century copy from the Red Book.

[4] The editors hold a different opinion. They say, Introduction, p. 8, 'The body of

for the critical study of the Dialogue this edition is indispensable.[1]

A large amount of materials illustrative of the work of the Exchequer is furnished by an important compilation made by an official hand in the early part of the thirteenth century. This is represented by two volumes belonging to the king's remembrancer known as the Black Book and the Red Book. The Black Book, sometimes called the Little Black Book, must be carefully distinguished from the Black Book of the Treasury of Receipt which contains the Dialogue. The Little Black Book,

---

the treatise contains one reference to a chapter heading, but examination will show that if this is anything but a gloss, it is a reference to a division of chapters other than that now existing.' The reference in i. 10 p. 202 is to a subject raised in i. 16 p. 208, though it is true that the full explanation of the matter in question is not given until the following chapter. But this is by no means the only reference. In i. 6 p. 188 and ii. 9 p. 225 'in titulo de summonitionibus' refers to ii. 1 pp. 210 f.; which in the new edition, p. 109, bears the title *Ex quibus et qualiter et ad quid fiunt summonitiones.* In ii. 4 p. 220 'in titulo de officio scriptoris thesaurarii' refers to the section *Quid ad Scriptorem Thesaurarii* in i. 5 pp. 185 ff. In i. 5 pp. 181, 183, and 186 'in agendis vicecomitis' may rouse a scruple; for the chapter *De agendis Vicecomitis multipliciter* is ii. 3, while the references are to ii. 21 p. 241 and twice to ii. 27 p. 246. But it is to be noted that the citations here are not of a *titulus* but of a subject, and *De agendis Vicecomitis* describes the subject of the whole of book ii. Cf. Liebermann, p. 7.

[1] I cite it as the Oxford edition, and its component parts as the Introduction and the Notes to the Dialogus.

which was written in the time of John, gives the best text of the Establishment of the King's Household under Henry I, and it sets out the *chartae baronum* or returns of services made by the barons in 1166 with some miscellaneous documents. There is nothing to show by whom it was compiled, but it is generally attributed to Alexander Swerford, who was treasurer's clerk [1] and became archdeacon of Salop and a baron of the Exchequer, and died in 1246. The only reason for identifying the authorship of the two books appears to be that the Red Book, which incorporates the chief part of the Black Book with very much more, is undoubtedly the compilation of Swerford and probably in part in his own handwriting. Swerford therefore at least deserves the credit of having taken up and transmitted the Exchequer tradition of his day. He is not to be compared in intelligence or knowledge with bishop Richard of London, and his comments on the records which he cites are often simple mistakes. If he was the actual transcriber of a part of the Red Book it must be confessed that he was a careless worker, and his proper names and numerals are not to be trusted. Still we are indebted to Swerford for preserving a large store of official information which we should not

[1] Alexander, the treasurer's clerk, of London, is mentioned in the 5th year of John: Rotuli Normanniae, ed. T. D. Hardy 1835, p. 108. A year earlier he appears as Alexander the clerk, of Winchester: p. 63.

otherwise possess. The Liber Niger Scaccarii was edited from three modern transcripts by Thomas Hearne in 1728;[1] it contains a good many errors, but most of them of a kind that can be easily corrected. The Red Book of the Exchequer was printed also from a transcript, but collated with the original, though not at all following the arrangement of the manuscript, under the direction of the master of the rolls in 1898. The preface is not helpful.[2]

The records of the Exchequer were at first preserved in the Receipt; but in course of time they outgrew this depository and were placed in four Treasuries, two in the Exchequer buildings by Westminster Hall and two within the precincts of the Abbey.[3] A catalogue of them was made in the latter part of the sixteenth century by Arthur Agard, who was a clerk in the Exchequer and became deputy-chamberlain in 1603.[4] But it does not appear that they were at all frequently consulted for any but official purposes. In the classical age of antiquarian learning—the age of Spelman, Selden, Dodsworth, Twysden, Prynne,

[1] I use the reprint of 1771.

[2] Mr. Round supplies criticism both of the text and of the preface of this edition in his Studies on the Red Book of the Exchequer, printed for private circulation [1898.]

[3] See bishop William Nicolson's English Historical Library, 2nd ed., 1714, pp. 208 f.

[4] Sir F. Palgrave, Ancient Kalendars of the Exchequer, iii. 451. Agard died in 1615.

and Dugdale, who all died between 1641 and 1686—it was the documents of the Chancery to which, after the chronicles, recourse was chiefly made. The reason for this was in part that the Chancery records were more accessible, under an experienced keeper, in the Tower of London: in part, that scholars found more convenient places for study in the incomparable library which Sir Robert Cotton had brought together in his house near Westminster Hall, which contained an abundance of materials for their purpose; and some of them worked in the Bodleian library, which gradually amassed a large number of transcripts of records. Though Agard bequeathed to him most of his store of Exchequer collections, when Cotton wrote a paper on a subject which they must have illustrated, it was An Abstract out of the Records of the Tower touching the King's Revenue; and William Prynne's Aurum Reginae,[1] published in 1668, is almost the first book in which the documents of the Exchequer were set out side by side with those of the Chancery.

In 1683, more than six years after its author's death, appeared A short Treatise concerning Sheriffs Accompts by chief justice sir Matthew Hale, who had been a judge in turn in all the three Courts, and was chief baron of the Exchequer

[1] William Hakewill, who died in 1655, also wrote a work on this subject, of which several manuscripts are preserved.

from 1660 to 1671. Its value lies not only in the lucid form in which the method of the account is stated but also in the fact that the author describes a system as he saw it at work which in principle had changed but little for centuries. Hale's little handbook must not be brought into comparison with the massive treatise written by Thomas Madox a generation later. Madox had the advantage of being himself a clerk in the lord treasurer's remembrancer's office and afterwards in the office of augmentation, and his History and Antiquities of the Exchequer is the product of ripe learning and of profound study of rolls and other records. It is a storehouse which will always be consulted with profit for the fullness, the precision, and the certainty of the materials which it contains. Its faults are first that, in spite of a careful classification and of a clear division made between the Exchequer before and after the accession of Henry III, the materials proved unmanageable in the author's hands; much information will be found in what is not obviously its proper place, and facts relative to the 'second period' are related under the 'first' and conversely: and secondly, that the author's extreme modesty prevented him from denying statements current in his day which his superior learning would have justified him in refuting. That there are also gaps even in Madox's wonderful equipment need not be concealed; but his book remains a monument of erudition of which any country might be proud.

After Madox we wait for more than a century before any work of importance was done in relation to the Exchequer. The appointment of the first Record Commission in 1800 followed by others down to 1831 led to the publication of a large number of reports on the contents of manuscript collections and of editions of unprinted materials both from the Chancery and the Exchequer; but the task of criticism and exposition came later. Hunter's preface to the Pipe Roll of 1130 is almost the only publication issued by the Commission which bears directly on our present subject. The masterly Observations on the Great Rolls of the Exchequer of Normandy, which Thomas Stapleton prefixed to his edition of the Rotuli Scaccarii Normanniae in 1840, stand outside the official series. They and the admirable treatise by Léopold Delisle on the Revenus publics en Normandie, printed in the Bibliothèque de l'École des Chartes between 1848 and 1852,[1] laid the foundations of the scientific study of the fiscal system of the Norman kings. Bishop Stubbs illustrated its parallel working in England in some ranges of its operation in the preface to the second volume of the Gesta Henrici,[2]

---

[1] 2nd series, v, vi; 3rd series, i, iii.

[2] The Chronicle of the Reigns of Henry II and Richard I known commonly under the name of Benedict of Peterborough, 1867.

and gave a compendious description of the whole in his Constitutional History of England.[1] For the Dialogue on the Exchequer Professor Liebermann's Einleitung, published in 1875, is of permanent value.

The foundation of the Pipe Roll Society in 1884 gave an impetus to the study in greater detail of the subject to which it was devoted; and to no one are we more indebted than to Mr. J. Horace Round, who in a large number of scattered papers has treated it with the sure grasp of an expert auditor and with an unequalled knowledge of the personal and territorial conditions of the twelfth century. Among smaller contributions I should mention an article by Mr. G. J. Turner on the Sheriff's Farm, which appeared in the Transactions of the Royal Historical Society for 1898,[2] and a modest essay entitled Compotus Vicecomitis, which was published by Professor Parow of the Friedrichs-Werdersche Oberrealschule at Berlin in 1906 and represents a great deal of laborious and careful work. The introduction to the Oxford edition of the Dialogue published in 1902 has the special merit of having been written by men who by their official position lived in constant touch with the records. Its scholarly cautiousness commands respect, and though not professing to give a complete description of the Exchequer system, it is the

---

[1] § 126. [2] New Series, xii. 117–149.

nearest approach to such a description which we possess.[1]

In the following lectures I propose to discuss in turn the manner in which money was paid and the system of account; the source from which this system was derived and the organization by which it was carried out on the part of the central administration and of the local officers; finally I shall say something about the Exchequer as a Court of law.

---

[1] There are unfortunately a good many misprints, particularly in the references.

II

THE ANCIENT TREASURY

WHAT do we know of the way in which the king's revenue was paid and of the officer or officers who supervised its receipt before the Norman Conquest? Modern writers have had no difficulty about the matter: 'The King's "Hoarder",' says Freeman,[1] 'was as old as the king's "hoard". Under the Norman kings he appears under the Latin title of Treasurer.' But in fact the word 'hoard' is never found as a designation of the king's treasure or treasury, and 'hoarder' (*hordere*) is that merely of a land-steward;[2] it is, as bishop

---

[1] Norman Conquest, v (1876) 434.

[2] In the Anglo-Saxon Laws the meaning is clear. Athelstan ii. 10 forbids any one to exchange cattle without the witness either of the reeve or the masspriest or the landlord or the *hordere*. Similarly in Edmund iii. 5 (preserved only in the Latin of the Quadripartitus) no one is to deal with an unknown beast without the witness of the head-reeve or the priest or the *hordarius* or the portreeve. Athelstan ii. 3. 1, 2, prescribes certain penalties against a man who is privy to his slave's theft, and adds that the same rule shall apply to 'any king's *hordere* or one of our reeves'. A domestic regulation, Cnut ii. 76. 1 a, requires a housewife to keep the key of her *hordern* or store-closet, which the Latin translates *dispensa*. *Dispensator* was an equivalent of 'steward'. In the Anglo-Saxon version of the Rule of St. Benedict (ed. H. Logeman, 1888) *hordere* translates *cellararius* (cap. xxxi).

Stubbs clearly pointed out, 'not the name of a great official.'[1] The statement about the 'hoard' as well as the modernized name 'hoarder' seems to be due to Freeman; but the *hordere* was suggested by Kemble, who in his accustomed way mixes up a good deal of sound fact with unsupported conjectures: 'The names,' he says,[2] 'by which the Chamberlain was designated are Hrægel þegn, literally thane or servant of the wardrobe, Cubicularius, Camerarius, Burþegn, perhaps sometimes Dispensator, and Thesaurarius or Hordere.' He then describes his functions by the help of the account given by Hincmar of the arrangements of the Carolingian court in the middle of the ninth century, and proceeds to give a list of the persons whom he has found holding the office.[3]

For these he cites eight charters, six of which he admits to be open to suspicion. They contain the titles *hrægl þegn, burþegn, camerarius,* and *cubicularius.*[4] Florence of Worcester adds the name *dispensator.* I omit *stiweard,* which comes from a glaring forgery.[5] Lastly there is one mention of a *thesaurarius* found in a Wilton chartulary of the thirteenth century;[6] the person so designated appears in another authority under the Anglo-

---

[1] Constitutional History of England, § 126 in a note.

[2] The Saxons in England, ii. 104, ed. 1876.

[3] P. 105.

[4] This last is from a fourteenth-century manuscript.

[5] Codex Diplomaticus, no. 899.

[6] Ibid., no. 320.

Saxon name of *hrælðen*.[1] Kemble did not quote the one definite example of a treasurer known from early evidence. At the time of the Domesday inquest Henry the treasurer held Soberton, Eastley, and Nutley in Hampshire.[2] From the Liber Wintoniensis, a survey drawn up between 1103 and 1115,[3] we learn that he held lands in the city of Winchester in the reign of Edward the Confessor.[4] It is not however said that he was treasurer at that date. The title cannot be proved to belong to any one before the Norman Conquest.

The 'hoarder' then rests upon a mistake. The 'hoard' is never used to mean a treasury. The treasurer has no pre-conquest evidence. The only names that we can rely on are the Anglo-Saxon *hræglþegn* and *burþegn* and the Latin *camerarius* and *cubicularius*, though none of these is cited by Kemble from authorities at all near the Anglo-Saxon period. The Latin names however do in fact appear in genuine contemporary charters, and the English ones are attested by early evidence of a different sort.[5] They will help

[1] Thorpe, Diplomatarium Anglicanum, p. 170.

[2] Fo. 49 *a*.

[3] See Round, in the Victoria History of the Counties of England, Hampshire, i (1900) 527 f. The existing manuscript was written about 1150: see a facsimile given by the New Palaeographical Society, part ix (1911) plate 212.

[4] Domesday Book, iv. 539 *a*.

[5] Dr. L. M. Larson has collected the evidence in a valuable thesis on The King's Household in England before the Norman Conquest (Madison, Wisconsin, 1904) pp. 124–133.

us to identify the officers—for they were more than one—who had charge of the king's money matters and whose title survived until 1826. The *burþegn,* the servant of the king's bower or chamber, was the chamberlain. He was also called the *hrælþegn* or servant of the wardrobe. The Chamber was the place where the treasure was kept. To this day the Chamber of London is the financial office of the City, and the chamberlain is the treasurer. The distinction between public revenue and the king's privy purse was unknown, and all money that came to the crown may be presumed to have been paid in to the Chamber. The other name, that of the *hrælþegn,* is not less significant, because the Wardrobe from the beginning of the thirteenth century can be shown to have done a large amount of the financial business of the country.[1] The king's privy seal came in time to be the special instrument of its administration, and thus, though the offices of the Wardrobe were abolished in 1782,[2] the name of the Lord Privy Seal continues its tradition to the present day.

I have said that the Anglo-Saxon bower thanes or rail thanes were more than one. King Eadred in his will made gifts to three classes of high officers of 80 mancuses of gold, to the appointed

---

[1] T. F. Tout, in the English Historical Review xxiv (1909) 496.

[2] By the statute of 22 George III, cap. 82.

dish thanes, the appointed rail thanes, and the appointed birels (or butlers),—a warning against our assuming that the Frankish order of four single great officers of the household, the chamberlain, the seneschal, the butler, and the constable,[1] was imported into England. Of chamberlains we had more than one; there were two in the Treasury down to 1826. But the chamberlains were laymen, and when accounts came to be kept it would be necessary to have an educated man, a clerk, to supervise their drawing up. This officer is known later on as the treasurer. Henry the treasurer, whom I have mentioned as holding lands under Edward the Confessor, may possibly have borne that title before the Norman Conquest, but what that title was in Anglo-Saxon is unknown. I suppose he was one of the king's chaplains, and he may have had no vernacular name, any more than the other chaplain whom the Normans called the chancellor.[2] Even when the treasurer

[1] Hincmar, de Ordine Palatii, xxii, xxiii (ed. V. Krause 1894) pp. 17 f.

[2] This seems to be the explanation of the description of *Rægnbold preost* as *Raginbold cancellarius* or *canceler*. The evidence for his having borne the title of chancellor under Edward the Confessor is insufficient. The subscription *Raimballd cancelt* is attached to a grant by Edward the Confessor of Wargrave to the Old Minster at Winchester, Cotton Charter x. 17; but the document though in form a diploma differs from every known specimen of a pre-conquest diploma in the facts that it is written in Anglo-Saxon and that it once bore a seal. The handwriting points to the reign of William the Con-

acquired a substantial position, he ranked after the chief chamberlain and only received the same allowances so long as he was engaged in the service of the Court. This was how he stood in the reign of Henry I. It was only when the account came to take the first place and the custody of the money the second, that the order was reversed, and the treasurer ranked before the two chamberlains.

As for the manner in which the king's treasure was supplied before the Norman Conquest there

queror: see the Facsimiles of Ancient Charters in the British Museum, iv (1878) 37. In Domesday Book he appears as *Reimbaldus de Cirecestre* (fo. 63), *Rainbaldus presbiter* (fo. 166 *b*), *Rainboldus presbiter* (fo. 65 *b*). In two other places (fo. 56 *b*, 68 *b*) *presbiter* is an interlineation. In fo. 180 *b* the word *canceller* is likewise inserted above the line. Raegnbald is also mentioned in ten charters. Seven of these were known to Kemble, who marked five of them as suspicious: the other two come from the Codex Wintoniensis, written in the second quarter of the twelfth century (Codex diplomaticus, no. 891) and from the Cottonian MS. Tiberius C. ix. of the fourteenth and fifteenth centuries (ibid., no. 813). The other three were printed from a chartulary by sir Thomas Phillipps in Archaeologia, xxvi (1836) 256; one of them bears the rubric, *Carta regis Willelmi confirmantis totam possessionem Reinbaldi cancellarii*. I therefore doubt whether Rainbald can be proved to have been styled chancellor before the Norman conquest. Mr. Round however thinks otherwise: see Feudal England, 1895, p. 421, and The Officers of Edward the Confessor, in the English Historical Review, xix (1904) 92. Compare Mr. W. H. Stevenson's note, ibid., xi (1896) 731.

is no evidence beyond the materials incidentally given in Domesday Book. From these it results that, although many items in the revenue were paid in kind, they were computed in money: the value of the cattle or corn or honey was an ascertainable and ascertained value. Bishop Richard, who it must be admitted, is not consistent with himself on this matter, gives the traditional account of the system as he had heard it:

[1] As it has been handed down to us by our fathers, in the early state of the kingdom after the Conquest, the kings received from their manors not sums of gold or silver but only payments in kind (*victualia*) which furnished the necessaries for the daily use of the king's household. And the officials appointed for the business knew how much was due from each manor. . . . I have myself seen people who have seen provisions brought up to the court at appointed times from the king's manors: and the officials of the king's household knew precisely from which counties wheat was due, and from which various kinds of fleshmeat and horses' forage and other requisites. Now when these were paid according to the appointed manner of each thing, the king's officials accounted for them to the sheriff reducing them to a sum of money, as

for a measure of wheat for bread for 100 men	1s.	
for the carcase of a grass fed ox	1s.	
for a ram or ewe		4d.
for provender for 20 horses		4d.

The tradition thus recorded in the Dialogue may be verified in Domesday Book. It seems that the

[1] Dialogus i. 7 pp. 193 f.

duty of providing for the maintenance of the king's household for each day had at one time been divided among his manors. Some were charged with the entire *firma unius diei* or *noctis* as their yearly rent; others with half or three-quarters of such a farm; in other cases again several manors were grouped together to supply the same amount. That these provender rents were valued in money can be shown from some examples in Hampshire. In the time of Edward the Confessor Basingstoke, Kingsclere, and Hurstbourn paid one day's farm; the amount is not stated.[1] Broughton paid £76 16s. 8d., it is not said for what. But Barton Stacey and Eling are each separately charged with £38 8s. 4d., for the farm of half a day. Two other manors are described as worth £76 16s. 8d.[2] This sum is manifestly the amount at which the day's farm was accounted for to the sheriff; and the recurrence of so peculiar a figure as £76 16s. 8d. suggests that it is a modification of an earlier round sum. But what this earlier figure was it is hard to say. It cannot be an addition on account of deficiency of weight; for there is no number of pounds which added to an equal number of multiples of pence will bring out the exact sum of £76 16s. 8d.[3] One is led

[1] Cf. Spelman, Glossarium, s. v. Firma.

[2] The figures are collected by Mr. Round in the Victoria History of Hampshire, i. 401–403.

[3] Thus £75 with an addition of 6d. in the pound comes

therefore to suppose that this figure represents a larger sum reduced by an estimate of the depreciation of the coins. Now £80 diminished by 9½d. in the pound leaves exactly £76 16s. 8d., and this I suggest to be the earlier amount of the farm of one day. In the time of the Domesday survey the £76 16s. 8d. is found to be increased to £104 12s. 2d. not only in Basingstoke and its neighbours,[1] but also at Broughton, Barton Stacey, and Eling. Similar figures are found in Somerset: in two instances £106 0s. 10d., in two others £100 10s. 9½d., in one £105 17s. 4½d.[2] They defy analysis; but they look as though they represented a sum between £95 and £98 enhanced by payment by weight. However this may be, it appears that in certain definite instances the farm of one day or night amounted before the Conquest to something like £80, and after to something approaching £100.

This result is not impaired by the fact that in most cases the one day's farm was very considerably reduced. The original application having been forgotten, the amount was for various reasons

to £76 17s. 6d.; £74 with an addition of 9d. in the pound to £76 15s. 6d. The excess of 10d. in the one case, and the deficiency of 14d. in the other do not represent a difference of a halfpenny in the pound.

[1] This is not stated in Domesday Book, but in an inquest of 1274 in the Hundred Rolls ii. 220 (where the figure is given as £104 12s.), cited and explained by Mr. Round, Victoria History of Hampshire, i. 401 f.

[2] Round, Feudal England, p. 111: The Commune of London, pp. 71 f.

diminished in the same way as other payments were altered. In Oxfordshire the night's farm was £50; at Beeding in Sussex it had been in king Edward's time £95 0s. 6d., afterwards £50, and at the time of Domesday £10. All I am concerned to show is that this farm bears traces of having been at one time a nearly uniform sum, based upon a definite obligation of a payment in kind. But the commutation was generally established before the Norman Conquest. There is also evidence that the gross sums for which the sheriffs were responsible had been, at least in certain cases, compounded for by a fixed farm as early as the time of Edward the Confessor, and that the sheriff was authorized to deduct from the amount payable by him the annual value of lands which the king had granted away.[1] Whether therefore cattle or wheat or silver pennies were rendered at the Treasury, they were reckoned in money, and it is certain from Domesday that the money paid was required in many cases to be subjected to a test; that is to say, an additional sum of money had to be tendered in order to make good the deficiency shown by the assay. This mode of payment is called 'blank', and I shall have often to speak about it hereafter. I only mention it here because there has been a good deal of misunderstanding on the subject. In the Dialogue[2] it is

[1] See Round, The Commune of London, pp. 72 f.
[2] i. 4 p. 176.

stated positively that Domesday makes absolutely no mention of this form of payment, and this assertion was unfortunately repeated by bishop Stubbs.[1] But as long ago as Charles II's time the facts were perfectly understood. Sir Matthew Hale quotes the statement in the Dialogue that it was set on foot by Roger bishop of Salisbury with the comment 'though in truth it were much more ancient, as appears by frequent passages in the Book of Doomsday'.[2] The existence of such a system indicates a relatively advanced machinery at the Treasury. It requires not merely the officials of the Receipt, but also skilled workmen possessed of such chemical knowledge as was needed for the purpose of the assay.

In Domesday Book payments in blank money seem to have been made almost exclusively from the king's lands, where one would expect a strict system to be first adopted; and it has been maintained that no private landholders ever received payment blank and that any instance which appears to indicate that they did can be accounted for by special circumstances.[3] The most common mode of payment was by tale, *ad numerum*, but there are many examples also of payment by weight, *ad pensum*. The two methods might be combined, as when the counted pennies

[1] Constitutional History of England, § 126 in a note.

[2] A Short Treatise concerning Sheriffs Accompts, p. 22.

[3] Introduction to the Dialogus, pp. 33 ff.

were required to be twenty to the ounce.[1] If the coins were weighed, of course the payer had to make good the deficiency, which might amount to as much as 16d. in the pound:[2] if he paid by tale later usage suggests that a fixed deduction was made from every pound he paid; as soon as we have definite information we find the deduction to be uniformly at the rate of 5 per cent. or one shilling in the pound.

Another mode of payment is spoken of in the Dialogue as of earlier use than that by weight. This is payment at a fixed rate, *ad scalam,* that is by paying a vantage-money of 6d. in the pound in addition to the sum due.[3] It has been suggested that this plan was adopted in 1108, when the coinage was reformed, and that when a second reform was made in 1125 payment *ad pensum* was enforced.[4] Undoubtedly payment *ad scalam* is found in Henry I's reign, and seems to have fallen into disuse before 1130.[5] But I am not at all sure that it meant anything but blank payment, taken on an average, without going to the trouble of performing the assay. If in a particular place the money was found ordinarily to be pretty good,

1 Introduction to the Dialogus, pp. 34 f.

2 See an example from the Roll of 1130 in Round's Commune of London, pp. 91 f.

3 i. 7 p. 194.

4 Introduction to the Dialogus, p. 38.

5 Sir Matthew Hale indeed cited *ad scalam* from 'the ancient pipe rolls' (pp. 21 f.); but Madox (ix. 2 p. 188) could not find any instances of such payments.

so that sixpence of advance would suffice to meet the loss by the assay, it might be agreed to dispense with the test and accept the additional sixpence. In later times this was undoubtedly the case. What is certain is that there are two writs of Henry I referring to the same payment, one of which describes the amount as £25 *ad scalam* and the other as £25 blank ;[1] and that there can be no dispute about the exact amount is shown by the fact that when under Henry II the money was paid by tale, the sum demanded was increased by 12s. 6d.[2] As this was now recorded by tale the sheriff was the loser : he had to pay out £25 12s. 6d., but was only credited with a deduction of this sum less a shilling in the pound, that is with £24 6s. 10½d.[3]

But we possess in fact no evidence as to the manner in which accounts were kept of the monies paid, beyond the tradition reported in the Dialogue that the old name for the Exchequer was Tallies ; that is, that the method which preceded that of

---

1 They are enrolled among the Chartae Antiquae, N. 15 and 16 in the Public Record Office: see the quotations in Madox, ubi supra.

2 See Round, The Commune of London, pp. 85 ff.

3 Possibly it was this inconvenience which led to the advance being raised to a shilling instead of sixpence in the thirteenth century. Thus in the close roll of 19 Henry III m. 2 (Close Rolls 1234–1237, 1908, p. 150) Eleanor countess of Pembroke is discharged of £135 *blancorum, que extense sunt ad* £141 15*s*. The writ is cited in error by Hale, pp. 28 f., as of the 13th year.

counting on a chequered board was that of reckoning the cuts and notches on split sticks. There is no reason for doubting the antiquity of this system of tallies, which survived until 1826 side by side with a more modern system. But it may be doubted whether bishop Richard is correct in saying that the place of payment was called the Tallies.[1] At least the only example that has been noticed of a transaction which in later times would have been described as at the Exchequer is said to have been done in the Treasury.[2] It

---

1 'Although a table of this sort is called *scaccarium*, the name is transferred so that the court itself which is at the session of the *scaccarium* is also called *scaccarium*; so that if a man obtain anything by its sentence or if anything be appointed by its common counsel, it is said to be done at the Exchequer of such and such a year. But what is now called *ad scaccarium* was formerly called *ad taleas*:' Dialogus i. 1 p. 171.

2 This is a plea at Winchester in the Treasury, some time after July 1108 and before the summer of 1113: see Mr. Round's paper on the Early Custody of Domesday Book, in The Antiquary, xvi (1887) 9, and Feudal England, pp. 142 f., 1895. It is printed in the Chronicon Monasterii de Abingdon (ed. J. Stevenson, 1858), ii. 116, and runs as follows:

'Mathildis Angliae regina Roberto episcopo Lincolniensi et Thomae de Sancto Iohanne et omnibus baronibus Francis et Anglis de Oxenefordscira salutem.

'Sciatis quod Faritius abbas de Abbendona in curia domini mei et mea apud Wintoniam in thesauro ante Rogerum episcopum Salesberiensem et Robertum episcopum Lincolniensem et Richardum episcopum Lundoniensem et Willielmum de Curceio et Adam de Port et Turstinum capellanum et Walterum de Gloecestria et Herbertum camerarium et Willielis however possible that the Tallies may have been a popular name for it.

This Treasury was kept in the king's castle at Winchester.[1] Henry the treasurer had a house there even before the Norman conquest,[2] and afterwards he acquired three manors in Hampshire.[3] One of the king's chamberlains also held the manor of Hartley Mauditt in Hampshire by serjeanty at the Treasury. His ancestor William Mauduit possessed it in the time of Domesday Book.[4] He held also Porchester, 'where, under Henry II, we find treasure stored on its way to Normandy. One is tempted,' says Mr. Round, 'to see in this practice the reason why Porchester was held by the Domesday chamberlain of the treasury.'[5] His widow had 'a house outside the gate of Win-

mum de Oileio et Goisfredum filium Herberti et Willielmum de Enesi et Radulfum Basset et Goisfredum de Magnavilla et Goisfredum Ridel et Walterum archidiaconum de Oxeneford, et per Librum de Thesauro disrationavit quod Leuecanora manerium suum nihil omnino debet in hundredo de Perituna facere; sed omnia quae debet facere, tantummodo in hundredo Leuacanora facere debet, in quo hundredo habet ecclesia de Abbendona x. et vii. hidas.'

1 Chronicon Monasterii de Abingdon, ii. 116.

2 In Wenegenestret: Liber Winton. p. 539.

3 Domesday Book fo. 49.

4 In Domesday Book fo. 47*b* William Maldoit held with other lands Herlege (Hartley Mauditt), Porcestre (Porchester), and Seldern (Shalden).

5 Victoria History of Hampshire, i. 432. William Mauduit is not however styled chamberlain in Domesday Book.

chester with land in Fuller's Street and houses likewise '.[1] The lands went with the chamberlainship and were held afterwards by the two sons Robert and William.[2] The offices of treasurer and chamberlain, as we have seen, were closely associated, and for centuries to come every writ of issue from the Chancery was addressed to them conjointly. It was natural that they should have been endowed with land in the neighbourhood of the place where their duties lay.

The Treasury was much more than a storehouse of money and other valuables. 'Where thy treasure is, there shall thy heart be also' was appropriately quoted by the author of the Dialogue :[3] it was the very centre of the administration of the Court. There was kept Domesday Book to be referred to as evidence of tenure, and there early in Henry I's reign we find the whole court sitting to decide a dispute as to the dues of the abbot of Abingdon and deciding it by reference to Domesday Book.[4] Finance and judicature from the first, it may be believed, went together ; and we shall see hereafter that the association continued down to the reforms of the

---

[1] Round in The Ancestor, v (1903) 208, from Add. MS. 28024 in the British Museum.

[2] Ibid., pp. 208 f. ; The Commune of London, pp. 81 ff. For some time the lands and the chamberlainship were held by Robert's son-in-law William of Pont de l'Arche.

[3] i. 5 p. 177 and 14 p. 207.

[4] Above p. 34 note 2.

nineteenth century. In like manner another piece of evidence of about the same time does not certainly mark an innovation, but it is the earliest example that has been brought to light of a royal writ ordering a sheriff to make a specific payment in accordance with an enrolment. It was published last spring by Dr. J. Armitage Robinson, now dean of Wells, in his work on Gilbert Crispin Abbot of Westminster,[1] and runs as follows:

> Henry King of the English to Richard de Monte greeting. Cause the Abbot of Westminster to have 10 shillings of my alms, as it is in my rolls. Witness the Bishop of Salisbury at Cannock. And this every year. Witness the same.[2]

Here we have several features of interest. First, the king orders the sheriff to make a payment of alms such as those for which, when the pipe rolls are preserved, we find him regularly asking for allowance as a deduction from his farm. Secondly, the order was recorded on the rolls.[3] This may

[1] P. 149 no. 32.

[2] 'Henricus rex Angl. Ricardo de Monte salutem. fac habere abbati Westm' x solidos de elemosina mea, sicut est in rotulis meis. T' episcopo Sarum [thus printed] apud Canoc. Et hoc quoque anno. Teste eodem:' from a Westminster chartulary, Cotton MS. Faustina A. iii. fo. 79.

[3] In 1100 Henry I issued a writ to Eudo the steward and Herbert the chamberlain ordering that the convents of Westminster, Winchester, and Gloucester should have *plenaria liberatio* from him at his feasts and that their chanters should have an ounce of gold. But no reference is made to any roll: the authority is oral—'as bishop Maurice of London has borne witness

either mean that the great roll of the year which we call the pipe roll was already in existence, or else that the king's writs were already enrolled in a form of which we have no example before the reign of John: the former alternative is the more probable. Thirdly, the order for a single payment is changed into a permanent charge by the addition of the words *Et hoc quoque anno,* with the witness repeated.

I wish we could fix the date of this writ, which Dr. Robinson places approximately between 1110 and Easter 1116. It belongs to a time when the system of account had been reduced to roll; it was no longer a mere matter of comparing the cuts

---

that they had in the time of my predecessors (Robinson, Gilbert Crispin, p. 141 no. 18). Sir Francis Palgrave long ago pointed out that this oral witness is the primary meaning of 'record': Rise and Progress of the English Commonwealth, i. 145 ff., 1832. Compare the use of *recordatio* in the Dialogus ii. 20 p. 240.

As for Herbert he is styled 'the king's treasurer of Winchester' in a charter of about 1100–1108 (ibid., p. 146 no. 27), and described by the chronicler of Abingdon as *regis cubicularius et thesaurarius* in William Rufus's time (Chronicon Monasterii de Abingdon ii. 43): but he witnesses as *camerarius* (ibid., p. 52), and this is his title in the Winton survey (Domesday Book iv. 531, 534, 558). The Lansdowne MS. 114 fo. 55 (a sixteenth-century transcript among the Burghley papers) contains a record of the inspection of a charter of Henry I in *rotulo regis* under Henry II; but Mr. Round thinks that this reference may be to Roll N. of the Chartae Antiquae at the Public Record Office written in Henry II's time (The Commune of London, p. 88), from which the charter is printed by Madox ix. 2 p. 188 *r*.

and notches on tallies. About the same time there emerges the name *scaccarium* or Exchequer: it is in a writ of Henry I to Roger bishop of Salisbury and the barons of the Exchequer ratifying a gift which his queen Matilda had made to the canons of Holy Trinity in London from the £25 blank which the king had given her from the farm of the city of Exeter. The document is earlier than May 1118, when queen Matilda died. The witness is Geoffrey of Clinton,[1] who had been at the Court in 1115 or earlier,[2] and who is found somewhat later, after the king's second marriage in 1121, to have been treasurer and chamberlain.[3] As we have found the king's court in session at the Treasury, so we now find the barons of the Exchequer entrusted with judicial powers. The king commands bishop Richard Belmeis of London 'to do full right to the abbot of Westminster as touching the men who broke into his church of Winton [Wenington, Essex] by arms at night. And unless you do it, my barons of the Exchequer will cause it to be done, that I hear no complaint thereof for default of right'.[4]

---

1 Madox, l. c., from Chartae Antiquae N. 16.

2 He witnesses with Ranulf the chancellor and R. Basset a charter of Henry I printed by Dr. Robinson, p. 147 no. 29 from the Westminster Chartulary D. fo. 516 *b*.

3 Madox, p. 40 *a*, from Chartae Antiquae OO. 12.

4 'Henricus rex Angl' Ricardo episcopo de Lundon' sal'. Mando tibi ut facias plenum rectum abbati Westm' de hominibus qui fregerunt ecclesiam suam de Winton'

The subject of the judicature at the Exchequer will come before us at a later stage.[1] Here I only mention it in connexion with the appearance of the word at a date not later than 1118. The word indicates a revolution in the method of auditing the accounts ; it means the introduction of a precise system of calculation worked out by counters on a chequered table and recorded on rolls.[2]

---

noctu et armis. et nisi feceris, barones mei de scaccario faciant fieri, ne audiam clamorem inde pro penuria recti : ' Robinson, p. 148 n. 31, from MS. Faustina A. iii. fo. 74. The witness is unfortunately omitted, and the editor gives the wide margin of date 1108–1127. Madox could not, ' upon diligent search, find the original writ in the repository of the church of Westminster,' iv. 5 p. 121, and printed it from the Cottonian MS., vi. 2 p. 141 *a*. It is also given by Stapleton.

[1] See below, chapter viii.

[2] When Mr. Round says in The Commune of London, pp. 80 f., that ' the change from the " Treasury " to the " Exchequer " was . . . a gradual process ', he appears to mean that the word Exchequer only came gradually into use as denoting the place of payment as well as the place of audit. And this is shown by the instances, given in his Calendar of Documents relating to France, i. 354 f., which describe the grants made to the monks of Tiron. First Henry I between 1114 and 1120 gave them 15 marks a year to be received *de thesauro meo in festo s. Michaelis Wintonie*. Then the empress Matilda in July 1141 confirmed this *de thesauro Wintoniensi*, adding 5 marks ; the whole to be paid *de firma Wintoniensi*. In 1152–1154 Henry duke of the Normans confirmed the same grant *de thesauro Wintonie*. Finally in 1156–7 Henry went back to the original 15 marks, which was made payable from his treasury at the Exchequer. Mr. Round states clearly in The Commune of London, pp. 74 f., the precise meaning

Thenceforward the Treasury was limited to the payment and storage of money; the business of account and the higher work of judicature passed to the Exchequer.

---

of the introduction of the Exchequer, and that introduction must have been a definite act which operated at a definite date.

III

THE RECKONING OF THE EXCHEQUER

NOTHING is more difficult to explain than a system so familiar that most of us never think at all about it. Yet our decimal system of arithmetic is the result of a long system of development. At an early time the scientific treatment of numbers was a part of geometry: 'the results of the fifth book' of Euclid 'in which the theory of proportion is considered apply to any magnitudes, and therefore are true of numbers as well as of geometrical magnitudes'.[1] When in the first century of our era geometrical demonstrations were abandoned by Nicomachus, arithmetic was reduced to 'the study of the properties of numbers, and particularly of their ratios'.[2] The work of Nicomachus formed the basis of that of Boethius four hundred years later; and this became the accepted text-book of the middle ages in the west. But the theory of numbers, ratio, proportion, and the progressions will not help you to 'do sums'. Ordinary practical calculations were not performed

---

[1] W. W. Rouse Ball, A Short Account of the History of Mathematics (3rd ed. 1901) pp. 60 f.

[2] Ibid., p. 98; cf. M. Cantor, Vorlesungen über Geschichte der Mathematik (2nd ed., Leipzig 1894) i. 400 ff.

in writing, though the results were written down. The calculation was done by means of a sanded floor or table called an abacus, afterwards by means of a tablecloth marked in squares or by means of a frame containing a number of counters strung on wires.

The reasons for this mechanical appliance were two-fold. First, the rudiments of calculation were considered to be things which were necessary to be taught to children but were undeserving of scientific discussion. In the second place it was practically impossible to perform an elementary arithmetical calculation in writing by means of the Greek or Roman numerals. It was not merely that their figures were cumbrous, but also that their decimal system was defective in that it lacked the essential element of zero, which did not come into the west from the Arabs until a late date.[1] Now the abacus supplied a simple means for addition and subtraction. If the floor was sanded the calculator made columns[2] of grooves

---

[1] Richer's statement, Hist. iii. 54, that Gerbert employed nine *notae* for his calculations is remarkably confirmed by Dr. N. Bubnov's proof that the treatise on geometry attributed to Boethius, in which nine figures nearly resembling the Arabic numerals appear, is a forgery of the eleventh century, which so far as the abacus is concerned, is based upon Gerbert. See his edition of Gerbert's Opera mathematica (Berlin 1899), especially the notes on pp. 157 f., 188 ff. But there is no trace of zero here.

[2] There is evidence of an abacus with horizontal lines,

with a stick and placed as many counters in each as he required. If he used a chequered cloth, the counters were arranged within the vertical columns. Every column denoted a decimal stage: units, tens, hundreds, and so forth. The principle of the value of position was established.[1] Thus, when a column had no counter in it, there was nothing to count: the discovery of zero was for practical purposes anticipated.[2] But this was only on the

but that with vertical columns is the only one that need be mentioned in connexion with our subject: see G. Friedlein, Die Zahlzeichen und das elementare Rechnen der Griechen und Römer (Erlangen 1869) pp. 23, 48 ff.

[1] This is clearly pointed out in the Dialogus i. 5 p. 183, where the disciple says, 'Videre mihi videor fieri posse ratione calculandi ut idem denarius pro calculo missus nunc nummum, nunc solidum, nunc libram, nunc centum, nunc mille significet.'

[2] When zero was introduced into the Latin world the abacus was superseded by calculations with the decimal notation, which was then called algorism. It derived its name from the eminent Arab mathematician of the early part of the ninth century, Mohammad ibn Músa al Khuwarezmi, whose arithmetical treatise was translated into Latin in the earlier part of the twelfth century. Of this work, Algoritmi de Numero Indorum, a single manuscript exists of the thirteenth century in the University Library at Cambridge (Ii. vi. 5 fo. 102), from which it is printed by Boncompagni in the first volume of his Trattati d'Aritmetica, a work to which I have not been able to obtain access in the Bodleian Library or in the British Museum. But no one recognized the name of Al Khuwarezmi in its Latin form until M. Reinaud (Mémoire sur l'Inde, Paris 1849, pp. 303 f.) and Michel Chasles (in the Comptes rendus de l'Académie des Sciences, xlviii. 1057 f., 1859). Both Chasles (p. 1059) and Cantor (i. 671) suggest

abacus, not in writing. Hence the calculation was performed by a mechanical process, and the result written down afterwards.

To introduce this decimal system into England meant a great deal when we consider that the traditions of the country ran not on decimal but on duodecimal lines. The hide of land contained a hundred acres, but this was the long hundred of six score. The arithmetic table ran up not to a hundred but to *hundtwelftig*.[1] The pound contained 240 pennies. The pound's weight was 12 ounces. To adopt in the place of this duodecimal system one based upon tens and hundreds was in fact revolutionary. It was not a change that could have come in by degrees; it must have been definitely devised by some one. I venture with due reserve to submit a conjecture as to who it was that introduced the abacus, or at least

that the translation may be the work of Adelard. The translation of the Liber Alghoarismi de Practica Arismetrice by John of Seville, or perhaps John of Luna, belongs to the next generation (Cantor, pp. 750 f.). To speak of 'the period of the general introduction of "Arabic" numerals, coinciding perhaps with the use of the eastern "abacus"', as is done in the seventh volume of the Publications of the Pipe Roll Society, p. xviii, implies a misunderstanding of the whole subject. The abacus was not eastern, and it was the introduction of Arabic numerals that led to its disuse.

[1] See Mr. W. H. Stevenson's paper on The long Hundred and its Use in England, in the Archaeological Review for December 1889, iv (1890) 313-322.

the manner in which the abacus was introduced, into the English Treasury.

We must first enquire what books of rules existed for the use of the abacus. The first name we hear of in this connexion is that of that great man of science Gerbert, who ended his life as pope Silvester II. But he mentions that as a young man, perhaps about 970, he made use of a book on the subject which cannot now be identified;[1] and before he himself wrote, a commentary on the Calculus of Victorius which includes the abacus had been composed by Abbo of Fleury.[2] About the same time a treatise on the abacus was written by Heriger afterwards abbot of Lobbes.[3] These three men were contemporaries and were masters of the schools at Rheims, Fleury, and Liége. They died in 1003, 1004, and 1007. They wrote for the purposes of teaching, and dealt mainly with multiplication and division and fractions. It is commonly said that these treatises are based upon Boethius, but Dr. Bubnov has proved from an elaborate examination of the texts and of their transmission in manuscript that the book on geometry attributed to Boethius in which the

---

[1] See the preface to his Regulae de Numerorum Abaci Rationibus, in Bubnov, p. 6; cf. note 5.

[2] Bubnov, p. 197 and note 1. See Chasles, in the Comptes rendus de l'Académie des Sciences, lxiv (1867) 1062 ff.

[3] Bubnov, p. 205 and note 1.

abacus is described is in fact a forgery of the eleventh century compiled in a blundering way from various sources and borrowing the whole account of the abacus from Gerbert.[1] The influence of Gerbert in the century after him is shown not only by this forgery which sought to attach his work to a famous name of the sixth century, but also by the treatises of several other writers on the abacus, among whom Bernelinus and Herman the Cripple of Reichenau are the best known.[2]

At the beginning of the twelfth century two more treatises on the subject were produced by Master Ralph of Laon and by Adelard of Bath; and there is also a brief collection of Reguncule super Abacum, which was printed at Rome in

---

[1] Ibid., p. 188 note 23. Dr. J. Tropfke, in his Geschichte der Elementar-Mathematik (Leipzig 1902) i. 12 f., inclines to this conclusion in regard to the abacus contained in the Geometria of Boethius, but makes no mention of Dr. Bubnov's investigations.

[2] See Cantor, i. 825–834. An extremely interesting manuscript at St. John's College, Oxford, cod. xvii, written for the most part in several hands of the early part of the twelfth century, contains a number of abacistic works, including those of Abbo and Heriger, commentaries on Gerbert, &c. Dr. Bubnov gives a list of them, pp. lii, liii. Fo. 3 *b* was written in 1110, and the handwriting is unmistakably English. The manuscript belonged to Thorney abbey, where it may have been written: see for instance fo. 29. It contains Anglo-Saxon entries—one on fo. 7 *b* from Bryhtferð the monk of Ramsey,—runes, and not a few words well written in Greek characters.

1882 from a manuscript in the Vatican library[1] by Enrico Narducci, in the fifteenth volume of prince Baldassare Boncompagni's Bullettino di Bibliografia e di Storia delle Scienze matematiche e fisiche,[2] and is of special interest to us because, like Adelard's treatise, it is of English origin. Its author, Turchillus *compotista*,[3] dedicates his book to Simon de Rotol̄, apparently Simon of Rutland, who like him had learned his art from 'our venerable master William R.'; and William the writer places above all the calculators now living. Turchill gives the plan of the abacus, with the signs and names for the nine digits which were used for counters. 'These signs (*figurae*),' he says,[4] 'as *donnus* William R̹ bears witness, we have from the Pythagoreans,' that is from the forged Boethius,[5] 'but the names from the Arabs.' Turchill deals with the use of the abacus for the

[1] Cod. 3123, of the second half of the twelfth century.

[2] Pp. 135–154. I owe this reference to the kindness of my friend Mr. Haskins.

[3] The editor's attempt to connect the author with Thurkill who saw his famous vision in Essex in 1206 (pp. 128 ff.) is ill-conceived. Apart from the question of date, the Vision does not profess to be written by Thurkill, and is probably by Ralph of Coggeshall: see H. L. D. Ward, Catalogue of Romances in the Department of Manuscripts in the British Museum, ii (1893) 506–514.

[4] P. 136.

[5] See Bubnov, pp. 156 f., 195 and the notes. Turchill says (p. 150) that we have the name of one of the fractions of the as *non ab antiquis sed a predicto Guillelmo R̹ validissimo calculatore.*

practical purpose of working accounts. Thus he says,

[1] When you first approach the abacus, that is the science of the abacus, set out the debtors with their debts; draw three lines across the middle of the table lengthwise, and put the tokens representing each, that is the number of those who pay and the number of what is to be paid, and arrange carefully the sum arising from their multiplication. In the upper line put the debts, in the lower the debtors; and the sum proceeding from these amounts in the middle. For example: suppose there are 23 knights, and each owes you six marks. You want to know what total number of marks is made up of these small sums, that is, of 23 times 6 marks. In the upper line of the column of units, put a six for the 6 marks that are owing; and in the lower line put a 2 and 3, a 2 in the column of tens and a 3 in the column of units for the 23 knights, because they are the debtors.

The process which is given at length and occupies a large quarto page is a tedious one, but it brings out the required result, 138 marks. In another example [2] a pound is to be divided among 288 workmen; and each one is found to deserve a halfpenny and a farthing and a third of a farthing, or as we should say more compendiously five-sixths of a penny. The most interesting example occurs near the end:

Verbi gratia. Ducente marce sunt inter $\overline{\text{II}}^{\text{D}}$ hidas dividende, que sunt hide totius Eisexie, ut ait Hugo Bocolandie.[3]

---

[1] P. 137.

[2] Pp. 151 f.

[3] *Bocolaudie* in the manuscript.

'Two thousand five hundred hides are the hides of all Essex, as says Hugh of Buckland.' The figure is nearly correct: in Domesday Book Maitland made it 2,650.[1] But what strikes one is that Hugh of Buckland is spoken of as a living witness and in a personal way. Now Hugh is said to have been sheriff of eight counties, and Essex was one of them.[2] He was constantly employed during the earlier years of Henry I, but is not found mentioned after 1114 and appears to have been dead in 1115.[3] This would seem to fix the date of our treatise. It introduces us to two men in England interested in the reckoning of the abacus in the first years of the twelfth century, Turchill and Simon of Rutland, both disciples of the famous calculator William R. All these names are otherwise unknown to us;[4] but it is not impossible, as Professor C. H. Haskins suggests,[5] that the master may be William bishop of Syracuse,[6] to whom Adelard of Bath dedicated his treatise de Eodem et Diverso, as 'most learned in all mathematical arts'.[7]

---

[1] Domesday Book and beyond, 1897, p. 400.

[2] Chronicon Monasterii de Abingdon, ii. 117. Compare Mr. H. E. Salter's remarks in the English Historical Review, xxvi (1911) 490.

[3] See Robinson, Gilbert Crispin, pp. 138, 148, 155.

[4] The treatise is followed by a letter on the conversion of pounds into marks addressed by Turchill to one Gilbert. It is printed by Narducci, pp. 127f.

[5] In a paper which reached me after this lecture was in print and which has since appeared in the English Historical Review for January 1912 (xxvii. 103).

[6] From about 1104 to 1115.

[7] A. Jourdain, Recherches

Ralph's Liber de Abaco was published for the first time in 1890 from the only known manuscript at Paris [1] by Dr. Alfred Nagl in the supplement to the thirty-fourth volume of the Zeitschrift für Mathematik und Physik.[2] Unlike most abacists he condescended to treat of subtraction and addition as well as of the more difficult processes. He also used signs for the digits which, as drawn in our thirteenth-century manuscript, bear a close resemblance to the Arabic numerals. What is more interesting is that he has a sign ⊙ resembling zero, which he calls *sipos* (perhaps a corruption of ψῆφος) or *rotula*; but he used it only for multiplication and in a manner which, as his editor points out,[3] is not only superfluous but confusing for calculations on the abacus. Apart from this system of signs, which may have come directly or indirectly from Arabic sources, Ralph bases himself entirely on the traditional authors such as Gerbert and Herman of Reichenau.[4]

Adelard's Regulae Abaci are preserved in three

---

critiques sur l'Âge et l'Origine des Traductions Latines d'Aristote (ed. C. Jourdain, Paris 1843), p. 453.

[1] Formerly in the abbey of St. Victor, cod. 534, now in the National Library, Fonds Latin 15120. Chasles just notices the existence of the book in the Comptes rendus de l'Académie des Sciences, xvi (1843) 162.

[2] Pp. 85–133.

[3] P. 91; Cantor, i. 842. He used the sign as a mark to indicate the figure reached in a series of numbers to be multiplied.

[4] Cf. Nagl, p. 100.

manuscripts at Leyden, Paris, and Rome, from which the work was printed in 1881 by Prince Baldassare Boncompagni in the fourteenth volume of the Bullettino di Bibliografia e di Storia delle Scienze matematiche e fisiche.[1] Adelard cites Gerbert more than once, as the man *qui hoc opus nostris Gallis restituit et regulis succintim compositis illustravit*,[2] but he appears to rest principally on the book attributed to Boethius and on an anonymous treatise on fractions written perhaps in Gerbert's time.[3] I cannot however profess to have examined the relations of the work critically, a task for which I am not competent. All that concerns me is to show that he continues the line of abacists of the tenth and eleventh centuries.

Now Adelard left England towards the end of the eleventh century and studied as a young man at Tours, after which he engaged in teaching at Laon. He left Laon probably not later than 1109 in order to acquaint himself with the learning of the Arabs—he had already travelled as far as southern Italy, but now he spent perhaps seven years in oriental travel.[4] At least in the preface to his Quaestiones naturales he says that seven years have passed since he quitted Laon, but it does not follow that the whole time was spent in

---

[1] Pp. 91–134.

[2] P. 91 lines 23, 24.

[3] Printed by Bubnov pp. 227–244.

[4] See especially Mr. Haskins's valuable paper in the English Historical Review, xxvi (1911) 491–498.

the east. I must not here speak of the important work which Adelard accomplished in introducing large ranges of Arab science into the Latin world ; his translation of the astronomical tables of Al Khuwarezmi or his translation, also from the Arabic, of Euclid's Elements of Geometry. I only advert to his place as a leading pioneer in a process which altered the whole system of learning and teaching in western Europe, in order to fix the date of his treatise on the abacus. That work belongs to a time before he had come into contact with the oriental literature of science, and may therefore with little hesitation be assigned to the time when he was occupied in teaching, and probably in attending lectures too, at Laon in the first decade of the twelfth century.

Laon was then a famous place of study, perhaps for twenty years the most important school in the west.[1] It seems to have been specially frequented by mature scholars, such as were William of Champeaux, Peter Abailard, and Gilbert of La Porrée. For this reason, I take it, Anselm the theologian who gave the school its chief repute, was known as the *doctor doctorum*. But the younger students were not forgotten, and Anselm's brother Ralph, the writer on the abacus, besides teaching theology, gave instruction in the liberal arts. Laon had for some time past had a close con-

[1] Compare my Illustrations of the History of Medieval Thought (1884) pp. 111 ff.

nexion with England. Helinand, a clerk of Edward the Confessor,[1] was made bishop of the see about 1052 and held it for forty-six years until about 1098. It was apparently in his house[2] that William of Corbeil, the future archbishop of Canterbury, lived when engaged in the education of the sons of Ralph the chancellor of the English king.[3] Some years later the great justiciar, bishop Roger of Salisbury, sent to Laon his two nephews, Alexander and Nigel, afterwards bishops of Lincoln and Ely, and the younger of them treasurer. They were probably there during the time when Waldric, who had been chancellor to Henry I since 1103, was bishop of Laon; that is to say, after 1106.[4] If Waldric's pontificate was tempestuous and not altogether creditable, still the visits he paid to England[5] helped to keep up the connexion.

A striking illustration of the impress made upon

---

[1] Guibert de Vita sua, iii. 2 (ed. G. Bourgin, Paris 1907) pp. 130 f.

[2] Here I follow the late Mr. T. A. Archer, whose paper in the English Historical Review, ii (1887) 103–112, throws much light on the relations between England and Laon about 1100.

[3] See Herman de Miraculis sanctae Mariae Laudunensis, ii. 6, in Migne's Patrologia Latina, clvi. 977. Mr. Archer believed Ralph to be Ranulf Flambard, and it is known that Ranulf had two sons whom he was bringing up with a view to a clerical career about 1102: see Mr. Archer's paper, ubi supra, p. 108. But it is on the whole more probable that Herman, who wrote near the middle of the century, confused Ranulf with Ralph who was chancellor from 1107 to 1123.

[4] See Mr. H. W. C. Davis's paper in the English Historical Review, xxvi (1911) 87 f.

[5] Guibert iii. 4, 7 pp. 144, 155.

England by the school of Laon is furnished by a narrative of a journey made to this country not long after 1123 by a party of clergymen from Laon. The cathedral church had been burned down during the riots that accompanied the establishment of a commune at Laon in 1112, when bishop Waldric was murdered. Some of the clergy of the church at once set forth with their reliquary and visited various parts of France to collect offerings for the rebuilding.[1] When the money was exhausted, nearly twelve years afterwards,[2]

[1] Herman i. 3–13 pp. 967–972.

[2] Herman describes this visit as though it was paid in the year following the journey through France; the latter ended about St. Matthew's day, and the former began on the Monday before Palm Sunday: i. 13, ii. 1 pp. 972, 973. But in the interval between them the *templum* was *ex magna parte reparatum*. This requires a space of more than six months. It should be noticed that Herman inserts the actual report of the clergymen sent to England in their own words, and this report speaks of archbishop William of Corbeil as *nobis notissimus*. This cannot therefore be a mistake as Mr. Archer supposed, p. 105, but is a proof that the report was written later than 1123. This was remarked by Wilmans, Monumenta Germaniae, Scriptores, xii. 653 n. 2. There is no evidence connecting William with Canterbury before he was archbishop. It is probable that Herman when incorporating the report in his work found the dates of the days of the journeys inserted in a calendar, and erroneously inferred that they took place in successive years. The second journey was made not long after 1123, because it is related by Guibert of Nogent in two chapters (12, 13) which interrupt the sequence of events in the third book de Vita sua and appear to have been inserted in it at a date subsequent to that at which the rest of the work was written. It was certainly made before 1132 because the

they determined to send out a new deputation, this time to England, to collect a fresh supply of alms. Wherever they went they found a ready welcome, in Canterbury, Salisbury, Exeter, and elsewhere, because they came from a place associated with the memory of the great master Anselm,[1] whose disciples were found or had relations at all these places.

To sum up the results of our present enquiry, the system of the Exchequer is a system of reckoning based upon the abacus. Treatises on this subject were written at Laon, one of them by Adelard of Bath, who earned a great name as an expounder of mathematics and physical science. The school of Laon had an unequalled influence on English scholars, one of whom lived to be treasurer. And this influence was exerted precisely at the time when the system of the abacus was introduced into the English treasury. Let me add one fact: Adelard of Bath is known to have received a discharge from payment of the murder fine levied upon the hundred in 1130.[2] The amount of his discharge was 4s. 6d., and implies that he held a small estate in Wiltshire. Such exemptions were the rule in the case of persons in the employment of the Court; and if we infer

travellers found, apparently at Glastonbury, an old Laon student Agardus, or Algarus, who became bishop of Coutances before that year: Gallia Christiana xi (ed. P. Piolin, 1874), 874.

1 Herman iii. 6 p. 977; 12 p. 982; 13, 15 p. 983.

2 Roll of 31 Henry I p. 22.

that Adelard's service was connected with the Exchequer, the suggestion gains in probability when we remember that the Exchequer was in existence before 1118 and that Nigel or Neal, the future treasurer, a former student at Laon, was actively engaged in the business of the Court at least as early as 1126 or 1127.[1] In order to avoid misunderstanding I should explain that I am not claiming that the treatises on the abacus in themselves would help in working accounts. Addition and subtraction were too elementary to find a place in most of the treatises I have seen; the student was assumed to have mastered these processes already. But it was the practical familiarity with the instrument which was important, and it was the introduction of this instrument in the form of the Exchequer which made an epoch in the history of the English Treasury.

It has long been disputed whether the Exchequer came to England from Normandy or conversely passed to Normandy from England. If the arguments which I have submitted obtain acceptance, it will result that the Exchequer is a system of account rendered possible by a simple mathematical apparatus which Englishmen learned in France.

[1] The date, 1124, considered probable by the editor (p. 541) for the charter dated at London in the Chronicon Monasterii de Abingdon, ii. 164, in which Nigel appears as witness, is inadmissible, because Henry I left England after Whitsuntide in 1123 and did not return until September 1126.

It was established in England under a king who was also duke of Normandy; and in very few years it is found existing in Normandy. Until lately the statement of Thomas Stapleton and Léopold Delisle[1] that there was no evidence for an Exchequer in Normandy until the reign of Henry II held the field; but in 1899 Mr. Round printed a document which proved that pleas were heard before the barons of the Exchequer in Normandy about the year 1130,[2] and mentioned a judgement given by John bishop of Lisieux and Robert de Haia and many others at the Exchequer.[3]

This introduces a very interesting combination. John, who was a man of good education, had been archdeacon of Sées, when he and his bishop Serlo were compelled by the oppression of Robert of Belesme to flee into England in 1103.[4] He was

[1] Bibliothèque de l'École des Chartes, 2nd series, v. 268, 270.

[2] See his paper on Bernard the King's Scribe, in the English Historical Review, xiv. 417–430. The document is printed on p. 426. The description of it given by A. Heales, The Records of Merton Priory (1898) p. 10, abounds in mistakes.

[3] Unfortunately we cannot fix the date with precision to a time before 1130, because Robert of Évreux, whom Mr. Round identified with a man mentioned as dead in the Roll of 31 Henry I, p. 159, is more probably the treasurer of the same name and place, whom Mr. Haskins has found to have lived to be chaplain to Stephen. See his paper on The Administration of Normandy under Henry I in the English Historical Review, xxiv (1909) 225.

[4] Ordericus Vitalis, Historia ecclesiastica xi. 7, 31 vol. iv. 192, 274 f., ed. A. Le Prevost.

already well known to king Henry, who made him one of his chaplains and called him into his counsels.[1] John was thus, as Mr. Round points out[2], brought into constant association with bishop Roger of Salisbury and with the staff of officials who reorganized the administration of England. The connexion was not broken when archdeacon John became bishop of Lisieux in 1107. His nephew, also John and also archdeacon of Sées, is found hearing a plea in England in company with the keeper of the king's seal and other officials at a date before 1124 when he became bishop of Sées.[3] Thus we find the uncle trained in the English Chapel in England and acting as head of the Norman Exchequer about 1130, and we find the nephew holding rank in the English Court above the keeper of the seal before 1124. The process is from England to Normandy, not from Normandy to England.

This discovery, I believe, sets the facts in their true relation ; but it would not be proper that I should pass over in silence the statements in the Dialogue which deal with the subject. The Exchequer, says bishop Richard,

[4] is said to have taken its origin from the very conquest of the kingdom by king William, though its principle is

---

[1] 'Inter praecipuos regis capellanos computatus est, atque ad regalia inter familiares consilia saepe accitus est :' ibid., p. 275.

[2] Ubi supra, p. 427.

[3] Ibid., p. 428.

[4] Dialogus i. 4 p. 176.

derived from the Exchequer over sea. But they differ in many points and wellnigh in the most important. There are some also who believe that the use of the Exchequer existed under the English kings, and they adduce evidence for this view from the fact that husbandmen now worn out with years on those estates which are called crown lands—men whose memory on these matters is hoary—have learned from their fathers and know perfectly well how much of blank farm they are bound to pay for every pound. But this manner of knowledge relates to the payment of the farm, not to the sitting of the Exchequer.

Here I may observe that this remark shows that the author understood the point of the argument.[2] He is discussing the question whether the Exchequer is of Norman or English origin, and he remarks with perfect justice that the question whether in old times payment was or was not made with tested coins has nothing whatever to do with the question whether a particular form of board of audit of accounts then held its sessions.[3] The bishop continues :

But those who say that blank farm began in the times of the English kings are confronted by the fact that Domesday Book, which contains a careful survey of the

---

[1] *Sumpta tamen ipsius ratione a scaccario transmarino.*

[2] This was duly noted by Dr. Liebermann, Einleitung in den Dialogus de Scaccario, p. 109.

[3] When in i. 2 p. 172 he says of the Treasury and Exchequer, *una tamen est utriusque origo*, it may be doubted whether *origo* means more than 'basis' or 'principle'; for, he adds, 'whatever has to be accounted for in the greater Exchequer is paid in the lesser, and what is paid in the one is accounted for in the other.'

whole kingdom, and gives the value of all the estates both in the time of king Edward and in the time of king William, under whom it was drawn up, makes absolutely no mention of blank farm ; wherefore it seems probable that after that survey was made in the time of king William, the system of blank farms was established for reasons which I shall explain.

Nothing has so much discredited bishop Richard as his assertion that blank farm is not mentioned in Domesday Book.[1] That book was kept in the Treasury and was habitually consulted as evidence for the charges due from land. If the bishop, as we are bound to believe, rose to be treasurer from subordinate office in the Exchequer, he could not fail to have often referred to Domesday Book. He ought therefore to have been aware that, as I have had occasion to mention before,[2] blank money, money *ad arsuram,* and many similar expressions occur repeatedly. But the fact that a man had occasion to consult Domesday for particular purposes does not imply that he made a study of the book ; and he might frequently refer to it without noticing a matter which had no bearing on the subject of his enquiry. Still the fact remains that he committed himself to the untrue statement that blank farm does not appear in Domesday. The last editors of the Dialogue are so much troubled by the mistake that they resort to the extreme course of rejecting

[1] See the pungent strictures of Mr. Round in The Commune of London, pp. 65 ff.

[2] See above, pp. 30 f.

the passage in which it occurs as an interpolation. They point out correctly enough that besides being untrue, it destroys the continuity of the argument,[1] but I fear they are applying a standard of literary cohesion which few medieval writers would satisfy. However this may be, there is no doubt that bishop Richard regarded the practice of testing money as the invention of his uncle, bishop Roger of Salisbury, as appears from another passage of an historical nature which in one sense completes its statement, though in another it introduces something of a contradiction. I have already quoted a portion of it giving the tradition as to the manner in which payments were formerly made in kind,[2] but I must now read the whole.

[3] As it has been handed down to us by our fathers, in the early state of the kingdom after the Conquest the kings received from their manors not sums of gold or silver but only payments in kind (*victualia*) which supplied the necessaries for the daily use of the king's household. And the officials appointed for the business knew how much was due from each manor. Besides this, counted money came in from the pleas of the kingdom and from payments by agreement and from the cities and castles where husbandry was not employed; and this was used for the knights' pay and for presents to them and for other necessary purposes. This practice then prevailed during the whole reign of king William I and down to the time of king Henry his son; so that

[1] Notes to the Dialogus, p. 171, and Introduction, p. 33, where the word 'latter' is a slip for 'former'.

[2] See above, p. 27.

[3] Dialogus i. 7 pp. 193–195.

I have myself seen people who have seen provisions brought up to the court at appointed times from the king's manors: and the officials of the king's household knew precisely from which counties wheat was due, and from which various kinds of fleshmeat and horses' forage and other requisites. Now when these were paid according to the appointed manner of each thing, the king's officials reckoned them to the sheriff, reducing them to a sum of money, as

for a measure of wheat for bread for 100 men	1s.	
for the carcase of a grass-fed ox	1s.	
for a ram or ewe		4d.
for provender for 20 horses		4d.

But as time went on, when king Henry was engaged abroad or in remote parts of the country in putting down rebellion, it became necessary that he should have a sum necessary for his expenditure in counted money. And at the same time there poured into the king's court a complaining crowd of husbandmen, or—what was more disagreeable to him—often met him as he passed by, holding up their ploughshares as a sign of the decay of agriculture. So the king, moved by their complaints, acting on the advice of his councillors, sent through the kingdom men whom he knew to be wise and fitted for the purpose, in order that they might go round and inspect each manor with their own eyes, and then, when they had made a valuation of the payments in kind, reduce them to a sum of money. And they decided that the sheriff of the county should be responsible at the Exchequer for the total of these amounts; with this new provision, that he should pay at a rate (*ad scalam*), that is 6d. for every counted pound. For they thought that in course of time it might well happen that money which was once good might deteriorate [by use]. Nor were they deceived. In fact they were compelled to require that the farm of the manors should be paid not only at a rate but by weight (*ad pensum*), which could not be done except by adding a good deal. This rule of payment was maintained at the Exchequer for several (*plures*) years, so that you will often find in the old yearly rolls of that king the words 'In thesauro c. libras ad scalam' or 'in thesauro c. libras ad pensum'.

Meanwhile there arose a discreet man, far seeing in counsel, clear in speech, who quickly rose to the front, by the grace of God, in all the affairs of state. . . . He was called to the Court by the said king, and though unknown yet not unnoble he taught by his example

How poor estate may breed consummate men.

He then grew in favour with the monarch and with the clergy and people, and was made bishop of Salisbury. He filled the highest offices and honours in the kingdom and had very large knowledge of the Exchequer, which without doubt, as is manifest from the rolls, flourished under him exceedingly. From the drippings of his abundance I have received by tradition what little I know. . . . He then by the king's command took his seat at the Exchequer, and when he had been for some years there, he found that the method of payment employed did not fully satisfy the revenue, because although the system took account of the number and weight of the coins it did not regard their fineness. For it did not follow that if a man paid for a pound 20 shillings corresponding to a pound's weight, he therefore paid a pound of silver; for he might have paid in coins mixed with copper or brass, unless they were tested. In order therefore to provide for the advantage of the king and of the state, the king took counsel on the matter and ordered that an assay or test of the farm should be made in the manner which I have described.

In this passage bishop Richard gives a history of the development of the fiscal system, which is exactly that which we should assume on *a priori* grounds. From payments in kind we pass to payments in money, from *Naturalwirtschaft* to *Geldwirtschaft*; then as the coins are worn, they have to be made up by a vantage-payment of 6d. in the pound or else weighed; then as they are debased, they have to be tested. Blank farm therefore appears as the last and most scientific method adopted. Since however we know that it is found in Domesday Book, evidently we cannot ascribe its invention to the genius of bishop Roger. Indeed, in the first passage I quoted, the author speaks of blank farm as within the experience of men of great age, who had learned it from their fathers, a statement which takes one back beyond the days of the great bishop. His historical account therefore does not agree with the facts.

Thomas Stapleton, seventy years ago, insisted on the English origin of blank payments.

[1] Blanch-money and blanch-ferms were consequent on the monetary system of the Anglo-Saxons. With them a certain number of privileged moneyers in the principal cities and walled burghs had the right, on payment of a fee, to have dies cast, or engraved, for the purpose of coining; but as a check upon any falsification on their part, the mint in the royal city of Winchester was made the general standard for the coin of the country. . . . In Normandy the coin in general circulation was from the foreign mints of Angiers, Mans, and Tours; so that the same

[1] Observations on the Great Rolls of the Exchequer of Normandy, prefixed to his edition of Magni Rotuli Scaccarii Normanniae, i. pp. xv, xvi.

means did not exist of testing the money paid into the Treasury by a fixed standard.

This statement is substantially correct, though Le Mans after 1063 would hardly perhaps rank as a foreign city and there are some obscure traces of a coinage at Rouen.[1] Still, it may be accepted as deciding the question whether payments in blank money are of Norman or English derivation. There is no trace of any practice of testing money in Normandy. But this has nothing to do with the origin of the Exchequer in its technical sense. The assay is far older than the Exchequer, and the Exchequer first came into existence when the chequered table was arranged for working the accounts about the middle of the reign of Henry I.

Bishop Stubbs,[2] accepting Stapleton's conclusions, pointed to the fact, which I have noticed,[3] that in Domesday the farm 'is in many places described as settled in king Edward's time' as seeming 'to prove the existence of a central department of finance before the Conquest from which the peculiarities of the English Exchequer were derived'; and he considered this to dispose of the contention that the institution 'was bodily imported from Normandy'. In like manner he found no evidence to connect the Exchequer with Sicily. The name does not appear there and the

[1] Delisle, ubi supra, pp. 186 f.

[2] In a note to § 126 of the Constitutional History.

[3] Above, pp. 28 ff.

financial procedure is claimed to have a Saracenic origin. Bishop Stubbs was therefore inclined to trace any points of connexion between the systems of the two kingdoms to the presence of English administrators, such as Robert of Salisbury, the chancellor of king Roger, and Thomas Brown, who was employed both in Sicily and in England. The number of men from England—it would be premature to call them all Englishmen—who visited the South Italian kingdom, and who were employed in its service both in church and state, has recently been abundantly illustrated by Mr. Haskins.[1] But while it may be admitted that the Saracenic model was not preserved in Sicily unaltered, and while there are points of similarity between the Sicilian and the English systems, it would be probably unwise to press the analogy too far, especially since we have absolutely no evidence as to the form in which the Sicilian accounts were produced and audited.[2] All that can be said with confidence is that the *diwan* or *duana* which dealt with finance makes its appearance in Sicily at a date somewhat later than that at which we find the Exchequer established in England.

One caution should be added. If we follow Bishop Stubbs in believing that 'a central depart-

[1] England and Sicily in the Twelfth Century, in the English Historical Review, xxvi (1911) 435-443.

[2] Ibid., pp. 651-655.

ment of finance' existed in England before the Norman conquest, we are not to suppose that it was set up by Englishmen. Henry the treasurer of Edward the Confessor is shown by his name to have been a foreigner. And under the Norman kings the administration of the country was almost wholly in the hands of men who came from abroad. The great bishop Roger was a native of Caen, and among the leading officials of the twelfth century in England we shall hardly find one of English stock.[1] While therefore we join issue with Rudolf von Gneist in so far as he supposes the Exchequer to have been established in Normandy earlier than in England,[2] there is nothing to object to in his statement that

[1] Bishop Richard may have had an English mother: see Liebermann, Einleitung, p. 30.

[2] Das englische Verwaltungsrecht (Berlin 1867), i. 194, 201. It is unlucky that Gneist should have repeated the statement that an original roll of the Exchequer of Rouen of the year 1061 was produced in 1587; for Delisle long ago showed that the word Exchequer did not occur in a better text of the document cited, and that in any case the document could not belong to the time of William the Conqueror: ubi supra, p. 268. It mentions *livres tournoys*, which were not current in Normandy until the time of Philip Augustus: ibid., p. 187. Professor Heinrich Brunner, Die Entstehung der Schwurgerichte, Berlin 1871, p. 150 note 2, pointed out Gneist's mistake; but still maintained that the Exchequer existed in Normandy earlier than in England. He sought to account for the absence of any evidence in support of his opinion by the fact that few Norman documents are preserved before the middle of the twelfth century.

[1] the whole terminology of the Exchequer is a Romanized jargon, both the names of the officers, *justiciarii*, *barones*, *vicecomites*, *ballivi*, *balliva*, *serjeanteria*, and the names of the things dealt with, *amerciamentum*, *misericordia*, *finis*, *forisfactura*, *maritagium*, *custuma*, *prisa*, *relevium*, *tallagium*, *argentum blancum*, *catalla*, *feffamentum*, *tenementum*, *tenura*; as well as the terms of reckoning, *compotus*, *quietantia*, *talea*, *visus*, *computate*, *liberatio*, *deliberate*, *superplus*, *summa*, and of procedure, *summonitio*, *warrantum*, *breve*, *rectum*, &c.

This characteristic of our language is very well known; it has been fully illustrated by the historians of English law—'we must . . . go as far as the gallows if we would find an English institution';[2]—but it is desirable to repeat it in order that no false inferences should be drawn from the fact that the Exchequer is first found in operation on English soil.

---

[1] Das englische Verwaltungsrecht, i. 202. The passage had previously appeared in the author's work, Das heutige englische Verfassungs- und Verwaltungsrecht, i (1857) 41 f. The string of words is taken almost entirely from Madox, iv. 5 p. 127.

[2] F. Pollock and F. W. Maitland, The History of English Law (1895), i. 58 ff.

IV

THE TREASURY OF RECEIPT

I HAVE spoken of the Treasury as fixed at Winchester at a time before the Exchequer came into existence. It continued there long afterwards, for there is no ground for supposing that there were two Treasuries, one at Winchester and the other at Westminster. The truth is that the word *thesaurus* denotes several things. Primarily of course it means treasure. The king was constantly travelling from one place to another, and he necessarily required money to be supplied him for his expenses. This money, this *thesaurus*, we find, as soon as we have documentary evidence, he ordered to be transmitted from Winchester to various places, for instance to Southampton [1] or London [2] or Carlisle.[3] A good example occurs in the roll of the 28th year of Henry II (1181–2),[4] where £6 were paid 'for the hire of carts which carried the treasure from London to Winchester and part of the same treasure to Salisbury and again to Porchester, and for many businesses of the Treasury while the king was sojourning on

---

1 Roll of 7 Henry II p. 59.

2 Roll of 8 Henry II p. 35.

3 Roll of 4 Henry II p. 175.

4 P. 139.

the coast'. There is no question here of any temporary treasuries, but simply of furnishing chests of money for current needs. Such notices are of great interest for establishing the king's movements at a time when precise information from other sources is frequently lacking; but they tell us nothing about the removal of the Treasury but only of some money deposited in it.

In the second place *thesaurus* means a place where money and other valuables are stored, that is to say, strictly speaking, the Treasury at Winchester. But when the Exchequer was held as a rule at Westminster,[1] it was necessary that there should be a safe place for keeping the money which was paid in at the two yearly sessions of the board. This place also was loosely called the Treasury; but the author of the Dialogue, writing about 1178, seems to avoid the name, and designates it the Lower Exchequer or the Receipt. I take it that Lower Exchequer is a descriptive term employed by Bishop Richard for the purpose of distinction, but one which never acquired official currency. The Receipt is the *recepta thesauri*, the place where treasure is received; but the ambiguity of the word *thesaurus* led to its being translated in course of time as the Receipt of the Treasury. Later on it became known as

[1] There are exceptions. The Exchequer of Michaelmas 1164 was held at Northampton, below, p. 72 note 2. In 1170 it was at Winchester: see Round, Feudal England, pp. 503–508.

the Exchequer of Receipt or the Receipt of the Exchequer.[1]

Now this Receipt in the twelfth century only existed so long as the Exchequer was in session at Easter and Michaelmas. The *archa thesauri* was then brought from Winchester to the appointed place.[2] When the audit was concluded the treasure was packed in chests and hutches and sent to the Treasury at Winchester; and at Winchester the Treasury remained probably so long as the king kept his continental possessions,[3] when it was necessary to have a store of coins at a place convenient for their export.

In treating of the Exchequer however this central Treasury has a subordinate interest. It is the Receipt with which we are immediately concerned. But both Treasury and Receipt were under a common administration, that of the treasurer and chamberlains, who being principally occupied at the Board of Exchequer employed deputies to act for them in the business of receiving money. The staff of the office and the work done in it are fully described in the Dialogue.

---

[1] Madox viii. 3 p. 182.

[2] Thus in the Roll of 10 Henry II, under Hampshire, *Et ad conducend' archam thesauri de Wint' ad Lund' v. s. & viii. d.*, p. 25; *Et ad portand' archam thesauri ad festum sancti Michaelis ad Norh*[*ampton*] *vii. s. & i. d.*, p. 28.

[3] See Mr. Round's paper on the Early Custody of Domesday Book in The Antiquary, xvi (1887) 10 ff., from which I have borrowed some of my references.

[1] There is the treasurer's clerk, and there are the two chamberlains' knights. And there is a knight who may be called the silverer, because his duty is to take charge of the assay of silver.

This official seems not yet to have had a definite title : he was the weigher or, as he was afterwards called, the pesour.

There is also the fusor [or melter],[2] who makes the assay. There are also four tellers [3] to count the silver, and there is the usher of the Treasury and the watchman. And these are their duties. When the money has been counted and put into forels [or leather cases [4]] by hundred pounds, the treasurer's clerk seals them and records in writing the amount received, the name of the payer, and the reason for the payment (*quantum vel a quo vel ob quam causam receperit*).

The treasurer's clerk, it should be noticed, has no duties outside the Receipt, of which he draws up the roll. A fragment of the receipt roll of the 31st year of Henry II was printed in 1899, and deserves a closer study than it has received. From the skin on which the roll was written it came to be known as the pell,[5] and the treasurer's clerk continued

---

[1] Dialogus i. 3 p. 172.

[2] In modern times he was the surveyor of the meltings and clerk of the irons.

[3] In the roll of 1 Richard I, p. 178, ten tellers were employed in counting the tenths paid at Salisbury.

[4] *Foruli* are translated by Madox 'binns', but this is an ambiguous term. The forel was used down to modern times for keeping charters, and there are specimens of them in the University Archives.

[5] Madox, xxiv. 11 p. 739, mentions a specimen of the 9th year of Henry III.

under the name of the clerk of the pells down to 1834.[1]

He also inscribes [2] the tallies of that receipt made by the chamberlains [or rather by their servant the tally-cutter [3]], and he seals, if he pleases, not only the bags of money but also the chests and every forel.

Beside him sat the clerk of master Thomas Brown, of whom we shall hear more in the future, to make notes of receipts and expenditure.[4]

The duty of the knights, who are also called chamberlains, because they minister for the chamberlains, is this: They carry the keys of the chests; for each chest has two locks of a different pattern so that the key of one does not fit the other, and these men bear the keys of them. Every chest has round a fixed strap, which when the locks are closed is sealed on the top with the treasurer's seal, so that no one can obtain access to it without their joint agreement. Also it is their business to weigh the money after it has been counted and placed in wooden skippets[5] by hundreds of shillings, that there may be no mistake in the counting, and then finally to put them in forels by hundreds of pounds. If any skippet is found to have too little, no addition is made of the estimated deficiency, but the whole amount in question is put back into the heap of coins awaiting calculation. . . . Also the chamberlains make tallies of the monies received, and in common with the treasurer's clerk they pay out treasure by the king's

[1] 4 & 5 William IV c. 15.

[2] See the Notes to the Dialogus, pp. 167 f.

[3] Dialogus i. 5 p. 181.

[4] i. 6 p. 190.

[5] Some turned skippets are exhibited in the museum of the Public Record Office, but these were used for keeping deeds. See the Catalogue of Manuscripts and other Objects in the Museum, pp. 93 f.

writ or by order of the barons, but only after taking counsel with their superiors. These three officers [the treasurer's clerk and the chamberlains] are sent all together or in turn with the treasure when there is occasion [that is when the money paid in is removed to the Treasury at Winchester, or when it is taken thence to any place where the king may require it]. These three have chief concern in all things that concern the Lower Exchequer.

It is then explained that when money is paid by the king's writ the precise amount is paid and the recipient counts the coins. If there is any deficiency he reports the fact; the money is counted by the tellers and the balance made good. But if he has passed the door of the Treasury, no matter who he may be or how great the loss, he has no claim to compensation. The text proceeds:

[1] The duty of the four tellers is this: when the money to be counted is paid into the Exchequer, one of them carefully mixes the whole, so that the better and the worse coins may not be separated but mixed together so that they may balance the weight; and when this is done, the chamberlain weighs in a scale as much as is necessary against the Exchequer pound. If the number of pence exceed twenty shillings by more than six pence, the money is deemed too bad to be accepted; but if the excess is six pence or less, the money is taken and is then counted by the tellers by hundreds of shillings. If however the money is paid from a farm and is to be tested then forty-four shillings from the heap are mixed together and put into a purse, which is sealed by the sheriff, in order that afterwards a test, commonly called the assay, may be made.

---

[1] Dialogus i. 4 p. 174.

The pennies current in the twelfth century were generally far below the proper standard either of weight or fineness, and it was necessary to protect the king's revenue from loss through this cause. Two alternative methods are mentioned in the passage I have just quoted. One was to put a pound weight into the scales and to reject any money offered of which more than 246 pence were required to make a balance; any money which did not exceed that limit of deficiency in weight was accepted, but the sheriff who paid in the money was not given full credit for it, and when his account was settled, a shilling was deducted from every pound. This was the rule for payments by tale (*numero*).

The other method was that of the assay, which was performed by the weigher and the melter. The procedure for its conduct brings us at more than one point into the upper Exchequer; but as it was strictly a matter concerning money and not accounts it may be appropriately described here. I summarize the description in the Dialogue.

[1] The weigher brings the purse of 44 shillings into the Exchequer, mixes them up, and weighs the required number in the scales against a pound weight. He then counts the coins and puts 20 shillings into a cup, replacing the other 24 in the purse. Two pence are given to the

[1] Dialogus i. 6 pp. 190 f.; cf. Introduction to the Dialogus, pp. 28 ff.

melter as his fee.[1] Then the sheriff with two other sheriffs appointed to act with him repair with the weigher to the furnace where the test is to be made. The work is now taken up by the melter, who counts the coins and puts them in a cupel of red-hot ashes. He then reduces them to a liquid mass, blowing and purifying the silver. But he has to take care not to cease until the operation is complete nor to injure or destroy the metal by excessive boiling; for in the one case the king, in the other the sheriff, would be the loser.

If the silver was not sufficiently purified, it would be reported at above its real value, and so the revenue would suffer: if it was manipulated too much, it would be reduced below that value, so that the sheriff would receive less credit than was due to him. The process had to be carefully watched by the persons sent from the Exchequer to supervise the assay.

When the test is completed, the weigher takes it to the barons and weighs the ingot against a pound weight before their eyes. He then adds coins from the purse to balance the scales, and writes their number with chalk upon the ingot, as *Yorkshire: The pound burnt so many or so many pence.*[2] If the sheriff challenges the test as excessive, whether from overheating or from the infusion of lead,

---

[1] This fee long persisted. Madox, ix. 2 p. 191 *b*, gives an instance from the Roll of 10 John of £57 8s. being blanched by £5 0s. 7½d. At 1s. 9d. in the pound the deduction would be £5 0s. 5½d., but the melter received 2d. for his pains.

[2] The ingot was used for making plate for churches or for the king's service, or else sent abroad to be coined in Normandy: Dialogus i. 3 p. 174.

then another 20 shillings are taken from the purse, and a second assay follows.

This accounts for the reservation of 44 shillings, to allow for the possibility of a second assay, with four shillings over so as to give a margin for deficiency and to pay the melter's fee.[1] I leave it to the metallurgist to explain the part taken by lead in the process. A more practical question is, what the assay was intended to do: was it to reduce the metal to fine silver or merely to sterling with 18 pennyweights of alloy to the pound? On the one side it is argued that the Exchequer would endeavour to obtain as large an amount of bullion from the sheriff as it could: on the other, it is proved that the deduction for the assay, technically known as the 'combustion', varied from 19d. to as little as one penny; and if even in a single instance the combustion meant a loss of only one penny, it is clear that no attempt can have been made to reduce the ingot to fine silver.[2] The obscurity which without doubt remains in the description in the Dialogue may reasonably be explained from the author's admitted unfamiliarity with the details of the process of the assay.[3]

The usher's duties are next described. He has to

---

[1] The melter was not paid more than his single fee of 2d.: Dialogus i. 6 pp. 191 f.

[2] See the discussion of the subject in the Introduction to the Dialogus, pp. 30 f., and in Parow's Compotus Vicecomitis, pp. 20 f.

[3] *Nec sollicitus super hiis fui*: Dialogus i. 6 p. 193.

keep the door and to supply the forels and rolls and tallies and all the other small requisites, the wooden skippets, the knives for cutting tallies, the purses and straps, everything except the ink which by an ancient privilege was supplied, for a charge of 2s. at each session of the Exchequer, by the sacrist of Westminster abbey. It has been maintained that Westminster is here a mistake for Winchester,[1] and no doubt it is the sort of alteration that a later transcriber might easily make at a time when the Treasury had come to be settled at Westminster. But in fact the cathedral church at Winchester was unconnected with the royal palace, whereas the abbey church at Westminster was in origin the chapel of the palace ; and as the king's chaplains formed the writing staff of the government, it would not be unnatural that the ink should be supplied by their servant, the sacrist.

The last official mentioned is the watchman.

Then we are given a list of the liveries or allowances paid 'so long as the Exchequer lasts, that

[1] Notes to the Dialogus, p. 170. The argument is that the term *maior ecclesia* is inapplicable to Westminster. But Mr. G. J. Turner has pointed out, in the English Historical Review, xix (1904) 287, that it is used by William fitzStephen of conventual churches, and Mr. C. Johnson has found an example (ibid. p. 506) of its employment under Henry III with reference to Westminster Abbey. Mr. Turner, p. 288, showed that in the 4th year of Edward I the sacrist of Westminster received a sum of 40d. half-yearly for ink supplied to the Exchequer.

is from the day on which it is assembled until the day on which there is a general departure'. This includes some of the officials of the Upper Exchequer whom I would rather speak of in a later connexion. But the principle of the payments may be stated generally now. The laymen, who are knights, and have nothing to do with writing, because presumably they cannot read or write,—they have to do with tallies and things of that sort—receive eight pence a day; and the keepers of the keys, the deputy chamberlains, claim to be provided with horses and arms, in order that they may be able to perform their duties when they are sent with the treasure to its destination. The writers, who are all clergymen, are paid five pence; probably they also received emoluments as chaplains. The inferior officials have a correspondingly lower allowance. The four tellers receive three pence if they are at London; but two pence if they are at Winchester, 'for they are usually taken from thence.' The watchman has one penny, and a halfpenny for a light about the Treasury. The usher of the Receipt has no livery, but a number of incidental fees: two pence for every writ of issue, two pence for every forel, five shillings at Michaelmas for the wood of the tallies. It is also suggested that he is not so much an official of the king as a servant of the treasurer and chamberlains 'in keeping the door of their house'. The weigher and the melter stand also on a peculiar footing: the one receives a livery of twelve pence a day, the other of five pence.[1] The peculiarity of their position is that, though acting in the Treasury, they are not like the other officials deputies of persons in the Exchequer. Bishop Richard is not sure how to rank them: he thinks they belong rather to the upper than to the lower branch,[2] but admits that they have no appointed seats at the Exchequer.[3] Possibly they were at first local craftsmen who were given a higher rate of payment because their employment was only occasional. But they came to be provided for in the same way as all the other knights, below the rank of the great officers, who had their place in the Exchequer; that is, they were granted lands in serjeanty.[4]

An account translated by Madox[5] from a pell of the Receipt of the ninth year of Henry III shows how the liveries continued unaltered down to the thirteenth century.[6]

The liveries of the ministers of the Exchequer of the term of St. Michael in the ninth year of king Henry III

---

1 Perhaps this is a mistake for 4d., which is the livery received by the melter in 1181: Roll of 27 Henry II, p. 129.

2 Dialogus i. 3 p. 172.

3 Ibid. i. 6 p. 190.

4 For the weigher see Round in the English Historical Review, xxvi (1911) 724–727, and for the melter, Madox xxiv. 14 p. 741.

5 xxiv. 14 pp. 741 f.

6 In the following quotation I have used Arabic numerals and have reduced marks and multiples of shillings and pence into a common reckoning. I have also inserted the daily wages.

for fourscore days, to wit, from the feast of St. Michael until the Monday next after the feast of St. Lucia, including both those days :

To three scribes [5d. a day]	£5.		
To the two knights of the chamberlains [8d. a day]	5.	6s.	8d.
To John de Windresor [the weigher, 1s. a day]	4.		
To the fusour [5d. a day]	1.	13.	4
To Simon Druel[1] [5d. a day]	1.	13.	4
To the four tellers [3d. a day each]	4.		
To the watchman [1d. a day] and for light [½d. a day]		10.	

Before passing to the chamber of account it will be convenient to say something of the money in use in England in Norman times. The only currency employed was that of the silver penny, and the pound was a term of account meaning 240 of these pennies. The reckoning was based on weight, what we now call Troy weight : 'twenty pennyweights make an ounce ; twelve ounces make a pound.' But in money the values of the intermediate stages, as they became finally settled, were inverted, so that in the twelfth century, as now, twelve pennies make a shilling, and twenty shillings make a pound. But the idea of weight was not forgotten, and we often find mention of the ounce of silver meaning twenty pence. Eight ounces make a mark, that is 13s. 4d. But there

[1] He was the usher. In 2 Henry III William Druel had received the office ; Madox xxiv. 4 p. 720 *h*.

were no coins corresponding to any of these denominations. When about 1144–1147, in Italy, the treasurer of St. Ambrose at Milan wrote to one of the canons,

Duas marcas argenti, in IIII frusta [packets] divisas, per negociatorem .B. de Zurla tibi transmitto, minimum frustum una[m] uncia[m], aliud aliquantulum maius duas uncias et dimidium habet, tercium maius secundo IIII uncias, quartum maius aliis marcam habet et dimidiam unciam,[1]

he means four packets containing respectively 20d., 50d., 80d., and 170d. These proportions might be transferred to weights of gold, so that, the ratio of gold to silver in England being 9 : 1,[2] the ounce of gold equalled 15s., and the mark of gold £6. But neither the pound nor the mark nor the ounce was a coin, any more than the guinea is at the present day.

The Norman name for the English silver penny was *esterlin*. It is found as early as about 1100.[3] It was necessary to use a distinctive term, because the English penny was worth two pennies of Le Mans and four pennies of Rouen, Angers, and Tours. The meaning of the name is unknown,

---

[1] J. von Pflugk Harttung, Iter Italicum (Stuttgart 1883), p. 481.

[2] In Normandy in 1180 the ratio was $7\frac{1}{2} : 1$. See Delisle in the Bibliothèque de l'École des Chartes, 2nd series, v. 207.

[3] See a document of the abbey of Préaux, dated either 1085 or 1104, in Round's Calendar of Documents preserved in France, p. 111.

but it certainly has nothing to do with the Easterlings or German merchants, as most books tell us.[1] The word appears in Latin as *sterlingus* or *sterlingo*, and down to the latter part of the thirteenth century a sterling meant an English penny. Not unnaturally the pound of sterlings, meaning a pound's weight of 240 pennies, became shortened into the pound sterling; but to this day the word *sterling* has the specific meaning of English currency as opposed to any currency abroad. You cannot speak of a franc sterling or a dollar sterling.

The *obolus* was a halfpenny, but its meaning was sometimes transferred to the half of any specified denomination.[2] Under Richard I there is mention of a mark of gold *de obol*[*is*] *Musce* or *Muscii*,[3] which is made equal to 10 marks of silver. These weights must have been of unusually fine gold, but the name by which they are described has never been satisfactorily explained.[4]

---

[1] This derivation comes down from the antiquaries of queen Elizabeth's time: see Hearne's Collection of curious Discourses (ed. 1775), i. 10 f., 14 f.; ii. 317.

[2] The gold and silver obols mentioned in the Dialogus, i. 5 p. 183, were only counters used at the Exchequer to represent 10*l*. and 10*s*. respectively. In Normandy the obolus equalled 5*s*. of Tours: Delisle, p. 208.

[3] Madox ix. 2 p. 189 *k*.

[4] Mr. Joseph Jacobs, The Jews of Angevin England, 1893, p. 160, suggests 'money of Moscow or Muscovy', the payment being due from Benedict son of Ysaac de Russie appearing in the Roll

Occasionally a foreign gold coin, the bezant, was used for payment, but it was received at a conventional value. In the Dialogue it is mentioned under the name of *aureus*.[1] It seems to have been taken as worth 1s. 9d. in the reign of John;[2] this corresponds to 7s. of Angers.[3] But in Normandy its value rose to 8s. of Angers, and in England in like manner it is found under Henry III and Edward I to be worth 2s.,[4] the shilling sterling having the value of four shillings of Anjou. The bezant is generally said to be the Byzantine *solidus*, brought into the west through the dealings of merchants. It was sometimes called rhetorically a talent.[5] But it is possible that the word indicates also the ducat, which was first coined by Roger II

of 27 Henry II, p. 134. But Moscow was not founded until 1147. According to a paper prefixed to the Roll of 10 Henry II, p. xi, 'it is quite clear that this fine of some £6 sterling is an equivalent for half a pennyweight or 12 grs. of *musk* (that most costly of perfumes) bargained for by the crown.' But if sir Henry Yule is right (The Book of Ser Marco Polo, 2nd ed., 1875, i, introd., p. 68) in valuing a pound of musk at Venice in 1311 at £22 10s., so that a pennyweight would be worth 1s. 10½d., it is improbable that half a pennyweight could be taken at a value of £6 in England a century earlier. Besides, the statement seems to involve a mistranslation of the Latin.

1 Dialogus i. 5 p. 182.

2 Madox xxiii. 29 p. 711.

3 Delisle, p. 208.

4 *lii s sterlingorum pro xxvi bizantiis auri*, cited from the Originalia of 40 Hen. III. m. 4, by Madox, viii. 4 p. 183 *r*.

5 Ibid., ix. 2 p. 189 *i*. Cf. Stubbs, Itinerarium Regis Ricardi, 1864, p. 456.

of Sicily in 1140 and derived its name from the legend on it which read ' dux Apuliae '.[1]

Besides such foreign coins, ingots of the precious metals or pieces of plate were sometimes received at the Treasury at their weight. This was certainly the case in Normandy, and there are examples in England, as when in the 26th year of Henry II the sheriffs of London and Middlesex paid £9 5s. 4d. in pennies, 5 marks blank, 9 small rings of gold, and 3 gold clasps.[2] But these formed a special payment not rendered in a money value; it was the valuables seized from a woman convicted of clipping coin.

The money paid in was receipted by means of tallies. A tally was a stick usually of hazel wood, measuring in length the distance between the tip of the forefinger and the outstretched thumb,[3]

---

[1] King Roger forbade the use of *Romesinae*, money of Rouen; *et mortali consilio accepto monetam suam introduxit, unam vero, cui ducatus nomen imposuit, octo Romesinas valentem, quae magis magisque aerea quam argentea probata tenebatur*: Falco Beneventanus, Chronicon, ad ann., in Muratori's Rerum Italicarum Scriptores, v. 131 c. The type was doubtless designed to commemorate the king's investiture with the kingdom of Sicily and his son's with the duchy of Apulia. See A. Engel, Recherches sur la Numismatique et la Sigillographie des Normands de Sicile et de l'Italie, 1882, p. 67. The baseness of the metal, which was supposed to be silver, roused indignation and is said to have caused distress: Falco, p. 133.

[2] Roll of 26 Henry II, p. 154; also quoted by Madox ix. 2 p. 190.

[3] See for what follows the Dialogus i. 5 pp. 181 f.

about eight inches. It was bored near one end so that it could be filed on a rod.[1] The sum paid was denoted by incisions on the two edges of it. A thousand pounds was marked by cutting out the thickness of the palm of the hand, a hundred by the breadth of the thumb, a score by the breadth of the little finger, one pound by that of a swelling barleycorn, a shilling somewhat less, 'but so that the cut took out a piece of the wood and left a little furrow.' Pence were marked by simple incisions without cutting out any wood. If a thousand pounds were cut, no other mark was made on the same edge, unless the half, five hundred pounds, in which case half the wood was cut away from the space of the incision: you cut the breadth required for a thousand but only removed half the wood, making the cut lower down on the tally. 'The same rule holds if there are a hundred pounds to be marked and there is no thousand, or if there are a score of pounds, or a score of shillings which we call one pound. If there are many thousands or hundreds or scores of pounds to be cut, the same principle is observed: namely, that on the more open part of the tally, that is the edge which is directly before you after the note has been made, the greater number is cut, and on the other edge the smaller.' A mark of silver was indicated

[1] See Madox's quotation from a pell of the Receipt of 9 Henry III, 'for rodds for the tallies v s.': xxiv. 14 p. 742.

by the number of shillings and pence. A mark of gold was cut like a pound, but in the middle of the tally, not near the end as pounds were. A gold coin, presumably a bezant, was cut like a silver penny, but not obliquely but by a straight cut. Thus the distinction of gold and silver was marked by the place or the form of the cut.[1]

Such is the description of the tally given in the Dialogue. It may be verified and elucidated by existing specimens of the thirteenth century. If you hold a tally[2] in your hand with the thick part and the bored hole to the left, and with the note recording the name of the person to whom the business relates and the cause of the payment towards you, then you will find the cuts for the largest denomination,—whether thousands, hundreds, or scores of pounds, or smaller amounts,—on the lower edge near the right-hand extremity, and no other denomination will be cut on that edge. The lower denominations are all cut on the upper edge, with the pennies nearest the right-hand end. The thousand is distinguished by a curved incision; the other cuts are serrated.

When the sums paid had been cut on the two edges of the stick, and the name had been recorded, it was split nearly to the bottom, so that one part

[1] Dialogus i. 5 p. 182.

[2] All the specimens given by Mr. Jenkinson in the paper referred to below are 'stocks': in the case of counter-tallies the description in the text would have to be reversed.

contained a stump or handle, and the other only a flat strip. The larger part which was kept by the sheriff was the tally; the smaller which was retained at the Exchequer was the counter-tally or *recautum*.[1] The two parts were also called the stock (*stipes*) and the foil (*folium*), and later on we find the stock known as the *scachia* or *chacia*[2] from the Old French *eschace*, a 'stick'.[3] But either part spoken of by itself might be indifferently called a tally. The terminology has left a permanent imprint on our language. If you lent money to the Bank of England down to a hundred years ago, tallies were cut for the amount: the Bank kept the foil and you received the stock; you thus held 'Bank stock' of the amount recorded upon it. When the form of cheque was adopted, it was not indeed called a foil, but the part retained by the payer is still the counterfoil[4]; and the word 'cheque' itself goes back ultimately to the same root as 'exchequer'.

There has been difficulty in bringing the descrip-

---

[1] Dialogus i. 5 p. 178.

[2] Madox xxiii. 28 p. 709 *d, f*.

[3] The word is still preserved in the plural *échasses*, 'stilts.' The gender forbids any connexion with *scaccus*, 'a dummy,' as is stated in the Publications of the Pipe Roll Society, vii. p. ix, apart from the facts that the singular *scaccus* is not found and that the word has not been proved to mean a 'dummy'.

[4] In modern times 'counterfoil' or 'counterstock' was used also as the equivalent of 'foil': see R. Beatson, Political Index (3rd ed.; 1806), ii. 319 note.

tion in the Dialogue of the tally and the way it was cut into agreement with such tallies as are preserved; and the explanation is this that no medieval tallies which have been described until this year from actual specimens are tallies of the Exchequer.[1] Those, for instance, which are figured in the Introduction to the Pipe Rolls [2] are tallies made between the reeve of a manor and his tenants; and it is only by inadvertence that the editor speaks of them as 'made at the Receipt . . . in token that he was to be acquitted of the sums in question at the Exchequer'.[3] They represent a business transaction between private persons, and have nothing to do with the Exchequer.[4]

In order to explain the disappearance of the official tallies we have to pass to a famous piece of modern history. By a statute of 1783 [5] it was enacted that tallies should be abolished and 'an indented cheque receipt' take their place on the death or surrender of office of the two chamberlains, when their offices were to cease.[6] But these

[1] In the Archaeological Journal, lix (1902) 288–302, Mr. Philip Norman describes Exchequer annuity tallies from 1692 and gives specimens of the years 1705–1707.

[2] Opposite p. 65. One of these is shown on the back of the cover of the Oxford edition of the Dialogus.

[3] Introduction to the Pipe Rolls, p. 68.

[4] Other bailiffs' tallies of 1279–1280 are described by Mr. Norman, ubi supra, pp. 302–304.

[5] 23 George III c. 82 § 2.

[6] At the same time, subject to existing interests, the offices of the usher of the Exchequer and of the tally-cutter were abolished.

officers, Montagu Burgoyne and the earl of Guilford had been appointed only in 1772 and 1779, and they did not surrender their offices until 10 October 1826.[1] The tallies remained undisturbed until the statute of 1834[2] put an end to the old system of the Receipt, as that of 1833[3] had overthrown the sheriff's account and all that went with it—the lord treasurer's remembrancer with his filacers and secondaries, the officers of the pipe, of the estreats, and the green wax, and the foreign apposer. On 10 October 1834, we read in the Gentleman's Magazine,[4] 'The most ancient revenue department in the state, the Receipt of the Exchequer . . . terminated on the various accounts of the last quarter being made up.' What followed is well known. On the 16th the tallies were burned, and the houses of parliament were destroyed. On 22 October the privy council met to enquire into the cause of the fire, and was unable to decide with certainty how it arose; 'but the most probable account, from the evidence adduced, is that it originated in the flues used for warming the house of lords, which had been unusually heated by a large fire made by the burning of the old wooden Exchequer tallies.'[5]

Some years ago however a bag of tallies was

---

[1] J. Haydn, The Book of Dignities, p. 166, ed. by H. Ockerby, 1890.

[2] 4 and 5 William IV c. 15.

[3] 3 and 4 William IV c. 99.

[4] New Series, ii (1834) p. 528 *a*.

[5] Ibid., p. 482 *b*.

transferred to the Public Record Office from the Chapel of the Pyx in Westminster Abbey, and these proved to be true Exchequer tallies of the thirteenth century. I was permitted to examine them recently. They formed the subject of a paper read before the Society of Antiquaries last spring by Mr. Hilary Jenkinson,[1] and they confirm in a remarkable way the accuracy of the details set out in the Dialogue.

The manner in which tallies were used was as follows. The ordinary tally was a voucher for payments which would be received at the account without alteration or addition. But besides this there was a shorter tally which was called the memoranda tally, which served a provisional purpose. At Easter the sheriff paid into the Treasury a portion of his farm, but no accounts were enrolled ; but the tally then given him had to be examined by the tally cutter and compared with the vouchers for his disbursements. This might lead to the alteration of the sums recorded. Moreover the assay had to be performed. When this was done, the memoranda tally was destroyed and a tally of the full length given in exchange, and to this was tied a 'tally of combustion'

[1] This has now appeared in Archaeologia, lxii. 367–380. The present lecture was written before I received the copy of his paper which Mr. Jenkinson kindly sent me, but I have revised it in the light of what he has written and with the help of the facsimiles which he has reproduced.

recording the loss made by the assay. So the tally acknowledging the sheriff's payment was kept by him and produced at the Exchequer of Michaelmas when he paid in a further instalment.[1] The procedure is not very clearly described in the Dialogue, and as the memoranda tallies were destroyed at the time we have no means of supplying any additional explanation.

I now pass from the Receipt to the Exchequer, from the place where the money was paid in to the place where the accounts were audited.

---

[1] See the Notes to the Dialogus, pp. 175 f.

V

THE EXCHEQUER BOARD

In considering the composition of the board of officials which was entrusted with the audit of the accounts of money paid in at the Treasury, we must not be tempted into supposing that the organization of administrative departments had far advanced at the time when the Exchequer was established. The king had his Court and his Council, but the persons who composed them were very nearly the same. He had his Chapel, the chaplains of which formed the writing staff of the chancellor; but it would be rash to speak of the Chancery as already existing as a department of administration, still more of judicature. He had his Chamber, which in course of time became the Wardrobe; and above all he had his Treasury: but the steps by which the Chamber, as a more personal depository, was differentiated from the Treasury are obscure.

Our leading authority for the organization of the king's household is a famous document entitled the Constitutio Domus Regis, the Establishment of the King's Household, which was drawn up very soon after the death of Henry I and gives a detailed account of the officials of the Court with their stipends and allowances. It is in fact a record of what we should call the royal establishment made for the information of the new king, who would need to know what his household expenses might amount to, and who would wish to have the opportunity of making alterations in them. That the record was prepared for the service of Stephen is clear: had it been made in Normandy, with the empress at the head of affairs, we should expect a different title. Stapleton indeed said that it was 'compiled, it would seem, in Normandy'; [1] but the only reason he gave for his opinion was 'that the bakers were to have 40d. to procure a *modius Rothomagensis* out of the contents of which they were to bake the required number of loaves'.[2] To set up the bushel of Rouen as a standard does not imply that the household was settled there; indeed had it been, there would have been no need to call upon the bakers to spend 40d. in procuring the measure. The compiler of the Establishment had probably resided at the court of Henry I, which had been in Normandy during the last two years of the reign,[3] and he set out the

[1] Observations on the Great Rolls of the Exchequer of Normandy, p. xx. It is not true, as is asserted in the preface to the Red Book of the Exchequer, p. cclxxxviii, that he 'attempted to prove that it applies exclusively to the ducal household of Normandy'.

[2] Ibid., p. xxi, note 2.

[3] See Mr. Haskins's paper on The Administration of Normandy under Henry I, in the English Historical Review, xxiv. 228.

practice as he found it. The Establishment is preserved in two compilations of the thirteenth century, the Little Black Book [1] and the Red Book of the Exchequer.[2] The text is in many points faulty, but that of the Black Book is the better of the two.[3] I shall quote from it the parts which illustrate our subject.

The chancellor shall have 5s. a day, and one lord's simnel and one salt simnel, and one sextary of clear wine and one sextary of ordinary wine, and one thick wax candle, and forty pieces of candle.

The master of the writing office, 10d. a day, and one salt simnel and half a sextary of ordinary wine, and one thick wax candle and 12 pieces of candle. But king Henry increased Robert [the keeper] of the seal so much that at the day of the king's death he had 2s., and one sextary of ordinary wine and one salt simnel, and one wax candle and 24 pieces of candle.

The chaplains, the keeper of the Chapel, and the keeper of the reliques have the corrody of two men, and four servants of the Chapel have each a double portion of food,[4] and two packhorses of the Chapel,[5] each 1d. a day and 1d. a month for shoeing; for the service of the Chapel two wax candles on Wednesday and two on Saturday.

I pass over the remaining particulars concerning the provision for the Chapel service, as also the offices dependent on the steward and the butler.

---

[1] Vol. i. 341–359, in Hearne's edition.

[2] In the manuscript it stands near the beginning of the book, but it is printed on pp. 807–813.

[3] Compare Mr. Round's remarks in his Studies on the Red Book of the Exchequer, pp. 31 ff.

[4] See below, p. 124.

[5] Compare below, p. 99.

In what follows I omit the allowances of bread, wine, and candles.

[1] The master chamberlain is like to the steward in his livery [that is, he receives 5s. a day if he lives at home, but 3s. 6d. if he lives in the Household].

The treasurer is as the master chamberlain if he is at the Court and serves as treasurer.

William Malduit shall have 13d. a day and continually eat in the house . . . and shall have three packhorses with their liveries.

The porter of the king's litter shall eat in the house and have three halfpence for his man and one packhorse with its livery.

The chamberlain who serves in the chamberlain's place 2 shillings a day. . . .

The chamberlain of the candle 8d. a day. . . .

The king's tailor shall eat in the house, with three halfpence for his man.

The chamberlains without livery shall eat in the house if they will.

The ewerer shall have double food, and when the king makes a journey 1d. for drying the king's clothes, and when the king bathes 4d. except on the three feasts of the year.

About the launderer there is a doubt.

These entries show very clearly that though the Chamber comprised the office of treasurer it had by no means lost its primitive connexion with the personal service of the king. About 1126 the same man, Geoffrey Clinton, was both treasurer and chamberlain.[2] Next follow the constables and then the marshals.

---

[1] Liber niger Scaccarii, i. 352; Red Book of the Exchequer, p. 811.

[2] Madox ii. 8 p. 40 *a*.

[1] The master marshal, namely John, has like payment [to the stewards and constables]; and furthermore he is bound to supply tallies [2] for the gifts and liveries which are from the king's Treasury and from his Chamber, and he is bound to have tallies against all the king's officials, as the witness in all things.

Then we have a description of the four marshals who serve the king's household, with wages of 8d. Their servants if sent out on the king's business receive 3d. a day; otherwise they have only their board. The ushers, who are themselves knights, receive three halfpence a day with their board. The ushers who are not knights have only their board. The watchmen, the fireman, the usher of the Chamber, and the curtainer conclude the list so far as we need study it. What follows relates to the king's hunt.

In this miscellaneous crowd of people forming the royal household and ranging from great officers of state to scullions and slaughtermen, we can disengage the elements of an administrative system. There are six great offices, four of the holders of which we shall find to have their places at the Exchequer, receiving a uniform stipend of 5s. a day, though the treasurer only has his allowance so long as he acts in the Treasury. This distinction supports the view that the treasurer

---

[1] Liber niger Scaccarii, i. 354.

[2] *Dicas* in the Red Book, p. 812; the Black Book has *duas*. For *dica* in the sense of 'tally' see Ducange, s. v.

is a recent addition to the staff and does work which had been previously done by the chamberlains. The marshal supplies tallies for payments. Under the chancellor there is a master of the writing office whose stipend has been raised from 10d. to 2s. The chamberlain at the Exchequer receives 13d. The other stipends mentioned are those of inferior servants; but we may notice that the Chapel has two packhorses assigned to it, because there were not only the furniture of the Chapel but also the rolls and records which needed transport. In the same way three packhorses are supplied for the chamberlains, because they had to convey the treasure to and from Winchester. One officer who appears preëminent at the Exchequer is not named, that is the justiciar. He is not namen because he was in no sense an officer of the king's Household; he was the vicegerent of the king himself. The king might, and did, sit at the Exchequer,[1] but in his absence the justiciar took his place.

A comparison of the Establishment of the King's Household with the description of the session at the Exchequer given in the Dialogue, brings out plainly the essential features by which the two are connected; and the detailed account furnished by

[1] Thus Henry the Young King, in Roger Howden's Chronica, i. 228; and John, *qui praesens fuit super scaccarium* in his sixth year: Madox iv. 8 p. 129 *t*.

our later authority helps us to fill in the picture supplied by the record of the arrangements under Henry I. But first I must say something about the Exchequer itself. Bishop Richard calls it the Greater or Upper Exchequer, to distinguish it from the Receipt,[1] but it does not appear that it ever bore this name: in the records it is simply 'the Exchequer'.

I have already explained at perhaps tedious length the exact meaning of the system of reckoning denoted by the name, and it needs no demonstration that Exchequer or Scaccarium means a chess board, a board divided into squares.[2] When this board came into use it was natural that the counters placed upon it should sometimes be spoken of as chessmen, and the process of account be said metaphorically to be a game between the sheriff and the treasurer.[3] But this is a simple play upon words, of a type very common among medieval writers, and is not to be taken seriously. I should not dwell on the point were it not that it has been confidently maintained[4] that the Exchequer is so called not

---

[1] Dialogus i. 4 p. 176.

[2] In the Dialogue only the vertical lines, from the point of view of the calculator, are mentioned; but the horizontal ones must be assumed. Archdeacon Cunningham, however, thinks otherwise: The Growth of English Industry and Commerce during the Early and Middle Ages (5th ed., Cambridge 1910) p. 156 note 3.

[3] Dialogus i. 1 p. 171.

[4] See the Publications of the Pipe Roll Society, vii. p. viii.

from the board but from the pieces. Of course ultimately the Old French *eschequier*, of which *scaccarium* is the Latinized form, is derived from the game of *eschecs*, or *scacci*,[1] from the plural of which we have the English 'chess' and from the singular 'check'. Nor does any one doubt that the word is derived from the Persian *shah*. But the opinion that *eschecs* or *scacci* means the chessmen has no support until a date long subsequent to the establishment of the Exchequer.[2]

The Exchequer is described in the Dialogue as follows :

[3] The Exchequer is a rectangular board, about ten feet in length and five in breadth, which is set after the manner of a table against those who sit round it, and has on every side a ledge about four fingerbreadths high in order that nothing which is set upon it may fall off. And there is laid on the top of the exchequer a cloth bought at Easter term, not of any sort, but black divided by laths at intervals of a foot or a span—

'which custom of laying a chequered cloth there,' I may interpolate from Madox,[4] 'continues to this day.'—

Within the spaces are counters according to their values, as I shall explain hereafter. Now albeit such a board

[1] See the New English Dictionary, under *check*, *chess*, *chequer*, *exchequer*.

[2] The earliest example of *scaci* in the sense of chessmen given by Ducange comes from the poem de Vetula, which passed under the name of Ovid and was popular from the second half of the thirteenth century.

[3] Dialogus i. 1 p. 171.

[4] iv. 3 p. 109.

is called exchequer, the name is transferred so that the Court which there is during the session of the Exchequer is called the Exchequer ; so that if a man obtain anything by judgement or anything be appointed by common counsel, it is said to be done 'at the Exchequer' of such and such a year.

The table, I take it, was placed at the end of the room furthest from the door, much like the high table in one of our college halls, but not on a dais. Its size was sufficient to accommodate all the persons who were engaged in writing or supervising the rolls and in placing the counters for reckoning. At the head and foot of the table there was a longer bench which projected far enough down the room to provide seats for those whose duties lay outside the account, the constable, chamberlains, and marshal, and for the sheriffs with their clerks. The arrangement of the seats at the board was in principle this. The head of the table was occupied by the chief officers ;[1] on the long side facing the room were the persons in charge of the rolls ; opposite to them were those who performed the reckoning with counters ; and at the foot sat the sheriff whose account was being audited, with his clerk. The great officers of the Household who had their

---

[1] A breadth of five feet would allow room for only three persons, not for six as is shown in a diagram in sir W. R. Anson's Law and Custom of the Constitution ii. (3rd ed., Oxford 1907), part i. 173 note 1. The others sat on the bench projecting below the table.

places at the board, or their clerks acting for them, together with two personal nominees of the king, are distinguished as the *maiores* or the barons, to whom the decision of difficult questions was entrusted.

The description given in the Dialogue of the session of the Exchequer is very well known, but I must not for that reason pass it over, all the less since it has not always been correctly understood. I shall however abbreviate.

[1] First and foremost, by virtue of his office, there sits and presides the first man in the realm, namely the chief justice. With him sit by the mere command of the sovereign, and so with temporary authority, certain who excel in greatness and discretion, whether they be of the clergy or of the Court. They are there to decide rights and to determine questions that arise. For the special science of the Exchequer consists not in accounts but in judgements of all sorts. For when a sum which is demanded is set out and the sums which have been spent are placed below it for comparison with it, it is easy to find out by subtraction whether the amount is made up or whether anything remains over. But when a complicated enquiry is made about monies which come to the Treasury in various ways and are demanded in sundry manners, and are not required of the sheriffs in the same way, it is to some a grave matter to decide whether they have done amiss; and for this cause the science concerning such points is called the greater science of the Exchequer.

After this preamble bishop Richard goes on to speak of the office of the justiciar as the president

[1] Dialogus i. 4 p. 176.

of the board. He has the oversight of all that is done either in the lower or the upper Exchequer, and all duties performed there are ordered at his command. And he has this special right

[1] that he can cause the writ of the lord king to be drawn up under his [sole] witness, in order that any sum may be delivered out of the Treasury or that a sum may be reckoned to a man which is authorized to be so reckoned by the king's warrant ; or if he prefer, he may issue a writ in his own name under the witness of others.

That is, he can give authority for issues out of the Treasury and for allowances to the sheriff for what he had disbursed in the king's service. The justiciar sat at the head of the board, that is at the right-hand end, 'at the middle not of the bench,' because that ran down the room, 'but of the board.'

On his left sat the chancellor, if he attended, a man 'without whose consent or counsel nothing of importance is done or ought to be done'.

[2] To him it belongs to keep the king's seal, which is in the Treasury and departs not thence except when by the command of the [chief] justice it is taken by the treasurer or a chamberlain up to the Exchequer to execute the business of the Exchequer alone. When this is done it is replaced in its purse, and the purse is sealed by the chancellor, and then is committed to the treasurer's keeping.

Elsewhere however it is explained that the seal was in fact kept not by the chancellor personally

---

[1] Dialogus i. 5 p. 177. [2] p. 179.

but by his deputy, the keeper of the seal, of whom we shall hear more shortly.[1] It was also by means of a deputy that he had charge of 'the roll which is of the chancery', that is, of the roll known as the chancellor's roll, which was a duplicate of the great roll of the treasurer.[2]

> It is held by persons of authority that the chancellor is equally bound with the treasurer for all that is written on the roll, save only the entry of what is received in the Treasury.

The treasury officials alone can tell what money has been paid in; but the chancellor shares their responsibility for the correctness of the account.

> He does not indeed dictate what the treasurer is to enter on the roll; but if he makes mistakes he or his clerk is gently to reprove the treasurer and to suggest the proper words.

If the treasurer persists in his opinion, the matter is brought before the barons for their judgement.

On the chancellor's left, but not at the board, sit the constable, the two chamberlains, and the marshal. Their places might be taken by others, and there might be more people on the bench. These are officials who had nothing to do with writing but only with the mechanical business of witnessing documents, producing writs and tallies, and taking charge of delinquents. The constable joins with the chief justice in witnessing writs of issue and of

---

[1] i. 15 p. 207; see below, pp. 110 f. [2] Dialogus i. 5 p. 179.

discharge, 'for in all writs of this sort it is required by ancient custom that there should be two witnesses.' It may be doubted however whether this custom was observed. The earliest writ of issue known to be in existence, the original of which, I am informed, has lately been rediscovered at the Public Record Office—it was known, like most things, to Madox, who printed it [1]—bears the witness only of one person, a clerk of the Chamber.[2] Indeed we may take it that the presence of the constable at the Exchequer was not expected. Bishop Richard has to eke out his description of his duties by saying that it is his business, when the king's mercenary soldiers come to the Exchequer for their pay, to discharge their liveries with the help of his clerk and of the marshal. He had also to pay the falconers and hunt-servants. But this could only be at the Treasury, for at the upper Exchequer there were no dealings with money but only with accounts. It is added that in these duties some one else might take his place, since 'by reason of more important and urgent business he cannot easily be separated from the king'. The constable

---

[1] x. 13 p. 268 *q*. This writ, as the Editors of the Dialogus note, p. 182, was not witnessed at the Exchequer and must accordingly have been issued from the king's Court.

[2] William of Sainte Mère l'Église: see Eyton, The Court, Household, and Itinerary of King Henry II, pp. 284, 293, 295.

is in fact still primarily an officer of the Court; his nominal position at the Exchequer is a survival of the time when the Court was everything.

Of the two chamberlains I have already spoken in connexion with the Treasury of Receipt, at which their employment was so constant that their office was separated from that of the master chamberlain of the Household and they were known specially as chamberlains at, or of, the Exchequer.[1] Closely associated as they were with the treasurer they did not sit at the Exchequer board itself: 'the treasurer receives the accounts for himself and for them, and dictates the terms of the roll in accordance with the sums that have been paid.'[2]

Next the chamberlains was the marshal's place.

The duty of the marshal is to set apart in its forel the tallies for the debts which the sheriff has rendered [that is, of the tallies which served as vouchers of the amount already paid by him], which also are entered on the roll, and moreover the king's writs of allowance or discharge or grant out of monies for which the sheriff is summoned [showing the sums by which the total amount due from him was reduced]. The name of the county to which it belongs is marked on the forel, and the sheriff who makes account has to supply the marshal with it. . . . And if a debtor does not satisfy his summons and is to be arrested, he is handed to the marshal for detention; and when the Exchequer breaks up for the day, the mar-

[1] Cf. Round, The Commune of London, pp. 81–85.
[2] Dialogus i. 5 p. 180.

shal sends him, if he pleases, to prison for public custody: but he is not to be chained or thrust into a dungeon, but kept by himself above ground.

There is no record of any special prison arranged for this purpose. As late as the time of Edward I we find the marshal consigning persons to the Fleet;[1] but afterwards he had a prison of his own, that of the Marshalsea, which was the prison attached to the palace of Westminster, the prison of the king's bench. If the delinquent was a knight or of higher rank, he was not to be imprisoned.[2] A baron must take oath that he will not depart without permission beyond the bounds[3] of the town where the session is held;[4] and when the Exchequer of the term is over he is to be confined in a safe place in free custody until his case is determined by the barons. A knight is 'freely guarded, not in the prison but within the bounds of the prison house, under oath not to go away thence without the licence of the king or of the chief justice'.[5] When the sheriff's account, it is added, is finished, the marshal takes oath of him in public that on his conscience he has made the account required by law.[6]

---

1 Madox xxiv. 6 p. 728 *q*.

2 Dialogus i. 5 p. 181; ii. 21 pp. 240 f.

3 See the Notes to the Dialogus, p. 175.

4 But if he sends some one in his place, he is liable to imprisonment even though he is a knight: Dialogus ii. 21 p. 241.

5 ii. 21 p. 241.

6 i. 5 p. 181.

We now pass to the second bench occupied by those who sat with their backs to the larger space of the room. First sat the chamberlains' servant, either a clerk or layman, who cut the tallies.[1] His duties have already come before us when I described the way in which the tallies were prepared and dealt with. He had to adjust the sums entered on the tallies for the payment of the farm with the sheriff's other outgoings, and to make the counter-tallies. When he had checked the entries, he handed over the tallies to the marshal for safe keeping.

Next to the tally-cutter sat one or more persons to watch the placing of the counters on the board and possibly to take turns at the work. I use the word counters because, although the current pennies were generally used, they were only used as counters; and it is important to bear in mind that at the Exchequer no money, as money, passed. The setting out of the counters was done by the *calculator*, who held no particular office:[2] any one might be deputed for the purpose, and he performed his task *secundum consuetum cursum scaccarii, non legibus arismeticis,*

---

[1] Down to modern times the tally-cutter was the subordinate of the chamberlains in the Tally Court. He seems to be the *contratalliator* who receives wages at 2d. a day in the Roll of 27 Henry II, p. 136.

[2] He is not to be confounded with the *computatores* or tellers of money at the Receipt: above, p. 75.

that is by the use of counters, not by the rules of arithmetic. He sat at the middle of the table so as to have freedom for his hand, and, as the sums of money to be accounted for were read out, he placed counters in the proper spaces. Of these there were seven, the lowest for pennies being at the extreme right, next came shillings, pounds, scores of pounds, hundreds, thousands, and finally ten thousands. The *calculator*, or counter, began by setting out in a row the amount required from the sheriff who was in attendance; and then in lower squares the monies paid into the Treasury or disbursed by the sheriff by the king's order. If the payment was by tale the account was settled by simple subtraction subject to a uniform deduction of a shilling in the pound; but if the farm was paid blank the reduced value certified by the assay was reckoned net.

On the left of the calculator there was room for other persons if required; and then, in close juxtaposition to the accounting sheriff, at the foot of the table, was the place of an official of high position, called in the Dialogue the clerk who is over the writing office; in the Establishment of the King's House he bears the title of master of the writing office and is ranked immediately below the chancellor.[1] The holder of it in that earlier record was Robert de

[1] See above, p. 96.

Sigillo, so styled because he was keeper of the king's seal;[1] and a comparison of another passage in the Dialogue shows that the clerk of the writing office was also the 'bearer' of the king's seal.[2] Probably the office developed into that of the vice-chancellor later on in the century.[3] It was his duty to provide writers for the roll of chancery—that is for what we know as the chancellor's roll, the duplicate of the pipe roll—and for the king's writs made in the Exchequer and for summonses, and to overlook their work.[4] In other words he was in charge of the writing staff of the chancellor, but was not immediately concerned with the audit of accounts, a work which the chancellor controlled by means of his clerk, the *clericus cancellarii*.

[1] It may be remembered that the keeper of the great seal is to this day an officer distinct from that of the chancellor, though the post has never been appointed to since George II, and that it was possible for the two to coexist until the statute of 5 Elizabeth, cap. xviii, declared that he had 'the same and like place, authority, pre-eminence, jurisdiction, execution of laws, and all other customs, commodities, and advantages as the lord chancellor of England for the time being lawfully used, had and ought to have, use, and execute as of right belonging to the office of the lord chancellor of England for the time being'.

[2] In i. 5 p. 184 the clerk has to find clerks *ad summonitiones conscribendas*: in p. 181 the marshal receives the summonses against the next term of the Exchequer *a latore sigilli regii signatas*. This was obscured in the earlier editions by the misreading *latere*.

[3] See Stubbs's Constitutional History, § 121 note.

[4] Dialogus i. 5 p. 184.

Bishop Richard now returns from the lower side of the table to the head and tells us who sat on the president's right and on the upper side of the table. The seat to the right[1] was occupied by one who was not an officer of the Exchequer but sat there by special order, the bishop of Winchester, about whom I shall speak later on. Then on the upper side of the table[2] were ranged in order the treasurer, the writer of his roll, the writer of the chancellor's roll, the chancellor's clerk, and the clerk of the constable's office. The treasurer is here the principal person: he has to conduct the business both in receiving the sheriff's accounts and in the writing of the roll. He dictates the terms of the record, from which it is taken down in the other rolls. His roll has to be absolutely accurate, for

[3] it is of such authority that no man may challenge or alter it, unless it happen that the error is so manifest as to be plain to all; and even then it must not be altered except by the common counsel of all the barons, and in their presence while the Exchequer is still enduring: but the writing of the roll made in the past year, or even of the present year after the Exchequer is closed, no man may alter except the king.

---

1 Dialogus i. 5 pp. 178, 184.

2 In i. 5 pp. 178, 189, *secundae sedis, in secundo sedili*, is an obvious mistake, found in all the manuscripts, for *tertiae*. The head of the table is the first bench; the second is that where the counter sits; the third, where the rolls are written; and the fourth, that occupied by the sheriff.

3 i. 5 p. 185.

The writer of the roll, known in later times as the clerk of the pipe, wrote the great roll, the great annual roll, which we call the pipe roll. This I shall describe in another connexion.[1] Side by side with him sat the chancellor's writer, afterwards styled the comptroller of the pipe, who produced an exact duplicate of the roll for the chancellor's use.[2] Each of them received 5s. at Michaelmas term, to provide skins for the rolls and for the summonses and receipts of the lower Exchequer.[3] The chancellor's writer had also the duty of making out writs of issue from the Treasury, and writs of allowance or discharge, but only of payments or allowances authorized by the barons while the Exchequer was sitting. The writs here mentioned fall into two classes: there are writs of issue, or *Liberate*; and there are writs of allowance and discharge, or *Computate* and *Perdono*. Both were made out by the chancellor's writer in duplicate, and the counterwrits were kept by the chancellor's clerk. When the account was made, the writs themselves had to be produced as vouchers. Then the writs of *Liberate* were handed to the treasurer and chamberlains; and the writs of *Computate* and *Perdono* were placed in the charge of the marshal.[4] The reason for this distinction is the following. The

1 Below, pp. 150 ff.

2 The chancellor's rolls are preserved with some gaps from 9 Henry II to 3 William IV.

3 Dialogus i. 5 p. 187.

4 Ibid. i. 6 p. 188.

writs of *Liberate* authorized the payment of money from the Treasury; it was necessary therefore that the treasurer and chamberlains should preserve the writs as evidence of issue when their turn came to be audited.[1] The writs of *Computate* and *Perdono* on the other hand had done their work, which involved no payment of money but was only a matter of account; consequently it was sufficient that the marshal should take charge of them as he did of the tallies. The chancellor's writer also wrote the summonses for the ensuing term, afterwards known as the writs of summons of the pipe.

Just as the treasurer overlooked the work of his writer sitting next him, so the chancellor's writer was overlooked by his neighbour on his right hand, the chancellor's clerk. But he had a much more important duty in checking the sheriff's account.

[2] He examines carefully the roll of the preceding year until the sheriff has made satisfaction for the debts which are recorded in it and for which he is summoned. Moreover, when the sheriff sits at the account, after the sums appointed in his county have been reckoned up and set in writing, the chancellor's clerk receives from him his writ of summons, with the king's seal attached, and demands of him the debts entered upon it, calling out 'Render for this so much, and for that so much'. When the debts are satisfied in full, he cancels them [on the writ] by drawing a line through them, so as to distinguish between what has been paid and what remains to be paid.

---

[1] See below, p. 190. [2] Dialogus i. 6 p. 189.

He also keeps the counterwrits of what is done at the Exchequer. He corrects and seals the summonses, and has infinite labour, chiefest after the treasurer.

The chancellor's clerk was indeed a very important official, and as the chancellor was usually absent from the board, he rose to be a very great man. In the thirteenth century [1] he acquired the title of chancellor of the Exchequer and in course of time came to be the principal, and finally the sole, minister of the crown in the financial department. Yet to this day, once in the year he puts on the gown of a baron of the Exchequer when he prepares the list of persons from whom the high sheriffs of the counties are to be 'pricked' by the sovereign.

Last on this bench was the seat of the constable's clerk, but generally some one else took his place, for his only business at the Exchequer was to bring the counterwrits of those made in the king's Court into the Exchequer at the terms of the Exchequer, in order to verify writs of Court which might be produced there.[2]

The fourth bench, at the foot of the table, like that at the head, extended down into the room; it was the sheriffs' bench, and besides the sheriff and his clerk who actually sat at the board there were others waiting in attendance until they should

---

[1] Certainly by the 32nd year of Henry III; see Madox, xxi. 3 p. 580.

[2] Dialogus i. 5 p. 178; 6 p. 189.

be called upon to make account.[1] But beyond these, immediately facing the bishop of Winchester, sat another confidential person who held no office. This was Thomas le Brun or Brown, of whom I shall speak in a moment. He too had a writer who kept a roll, but as there was not room on the writers' bench for him he had a raised seat behind the treasurer's writer, from which he could look over the roll and take down what he required.

I now come to the two persons who attended the board and ranked as barons not by virtue of any office they held but by special order of the king (*ex novella constitutione*).[2] It will be noticed that they occupied corresponding seats at the head and foot of the table so that they could keep an eye upon the record which was being entered on the rolls. Of these two men one, Richard of Ilchester sat on the justiciar's right, and if, as probably became more and more the general rule, both justiciar and chancellor were absent, he sat

[1] In ii. 4 p. 220 it is said that all the sheriffs except the actual accountant were excluded; but in i. 5 p. 178 they are named in the plural. Probably those who sat below the board were deemed not to be technically present.

[2] I incline to the reading of the Black Book, *non ex officio*, in i. 5 p. 178, in spite of the fact that both the bishop of Winchester and Thomas Brown are evidently included in i. 6 p. 190 among those *qui ad maius scaccarium ex officio resident*. The king's command made their attendance an *officium*, but they held no specific office. The Oxford edition omits *non*; see the Notes, p. 173.

alone at the head of the board. In any case his position between the president and the treasurer was a very important one.[1] Richard is first found as a writer of the court (*scriptor curiae*) between 1156 and 1162.[2] He was then rewarded by the archdeaconry of Poitiers, which did not as a matter of fact interfere with his duties in England. In 1165 he sat among the barons [3] at the Exchequer. He was repeatedly justice in eyre, and in 1173 was made bishop of Winchester and in 1176 justiciar of Normandy. He was one of Henry II's most trusted ministers and was often employed on diplomatic missions. It is in connexion with him that the justices' roll first appears, and it has been suggested [4] that he introduced the practice of enrolling their proceedings. In the Dialogue we read that

[5] before his promotion, when he served in a somewhat

---

[1] Sir W. R. Anson, Law and Custom of the Constitution, ii. part i. 173 note, places him 'at right angles to the justiciar'; but the description in the Dialogue, i. 5 pp. 178 and 184, is clear.

[2] See Miss Norgate's article in the Dictionary of National Biography, xlviii. 194ff., where full references are given.

[3] This word is not used; but the phrase *assidentibus iusticiis regis* seems to refer to the first three names, among which is that of archdeacon Richard. Part of the text is quoted by Madox in the dissertation prefixed to his Formulare Anglicanum, 1702, p. xix, from the original among the muniments of Westminster Abbey. Richard appears among the barons in 1169, ibid., no. ccxci. p. 179: cf. Eyton, p. 130.

[4] By Miss Norgate, ubi supra, p. 195*a*.

[5] Dialogus i. 5 p. 184.

lower place in the king's Court, his trustworthiness and industry made him indispensable to the king's affairs, and he was alert and businesslike in reckonings and in the writing of rolls and writs. He was therefore given a seat beside the treasurer, in order that with him he might overlook the writing of the roll and all such matters. For the treasurer is distracted with so many and great cares and anxieties that it is excusable for him sometimes to fall asleep over his work.

At the opposite end of the table was master Thomas Brown, who had had a career in Sicily before he returned to his native country. It is possible that he went out with Robert of Selby who became chancellor of Sicily, and that a charter was given 'by the hand of master Thomas the king's chaplain' at so early a date as 1137.[1] He was certainly a member of the king's Court in 1143, and in 1149 is found engaged in the *diwan* or financial department of the administration. One may read his name in Greek and in Arabic in Sicilian documents.[2] According to the Dialogue[3] he was compelled to leave Sicily on the death of Roger II in 1154 and was invited by the English king to enter his service. The statement here made that 'he was a great man in the Court of the great Sicilian king and almost first in the

[1] For this and what follows see Mr. Haskins's paper on England and Sicily in the twelfth Century, in the English Historical Review, xxvi (1911) 439 ff.

[2] القايد برون, *μάγιστρο* Θωμᾶ *τοῦ* Βρούνου: S. Cusa, I Diplomi Greci ed Arabi di Sicilia, i (Palermo 1868) pp. 30, 313.

[3] i. 6 p. 190.

king's counsels' may be exaggerated; but the last phrase, *in regis secretis pene praecipuus*, very likely indicates that he held nearly the highest place in the fiscal department known as the *duana de secretis*.[1] From 1158 there are signs of his being in the king's employment; from 1160 to his death in 1180 he was in the receipt of 5d. a day from the farm of Hereford, the regular stipend of a clerk; and in some years he had in addition 5s. a day from Essex and Hertfordshire, the same amount as the vice-chancellor. Moreover from 1165, if not earlier, he was the king's almoner, and held this post until at least 1177. He was also a landed man, with a house at Winchester and four houses near Hereford.[2]

In these two persons, bishop Richard of Winchester and master Thomas Brown, I have long been accustomed to see the origin of the two remembrancers who first appear by name under Henry III.[3] The position of each at the board

---

[1] Cf. Haskins, p. 441 n. 49.

[2] Notes to the Dialogus, p. 173; Haskins, pp. 442 f. As there appear to have been more than one almoner, I doubt whether the appointment of Roger the Templar in 1177 necessarily involves, as Mr. Haskins holds, the supersession of Thomas Brown.

[3] The two were long without the distinctive titles of king's and treasurer's remembrancer. In the Liberate roll of 14 Edward I, m. 3, a writ is addressed *Nicholao de Castello uno rememoratorum scaccarii nostri . . . et magistro Odoni de Westminstre alteri rememoratorum eiusdem scaccarii nostri*: Madox, xxiv. 1 p. 714 *l*. The *rememorator*

enabled him, as I have said, to keep an eye on the writing of the roll; and Thomas Brown had a clerk who wrote a roll himself. The nature of this roll has been, I think, a little misunderstood. It has been suggested that it was an accurate copy of the rolls kept by the treasurer and chancellor,[1] but the statement in the Dialogue is that the clerk looks over the treasurer's writer 'and takes from him what he requires' (*et ab ipso quod oportet excipiat*[2]). This is not the way in which to describe 'an accurate copy'. It is quite true that we are afterwards told that if an error is made by Thomas Brown's clerk *in excipiendo*, it will be easy to correct it while the rolls are revised by making a comparison of all three; but it does not follow from this that the third roll contained everything that was written in the other two. In another passage of the Dialogue this third roll is said to contain 'the rights of the kingdom and the secrets of the king' (*regni iura regisque secreta*),[3] and this expresses, if perhaps in an unnecessarily grandiose style, very nearly what the remembrancers of later times wrote in their memoranda rolls: they recorded the sums due to the crown to make certain that they were not

---

thesaurarii is cited from the Lord Treasurer's Memoranda Roll of 26 and 27 Edward I: ibid., *o*.

[1] Introduction to the Dialogus, p. 27; Haskins, ubi supra, p. 443 note 61.

[2] i. 5 p. 179.

[3] i. 6 p. 191.

omitted by the treasurer, they noted business adjourned at the Exchequer, and a variety of incidental matters.

I do not for a moment suppose that the remembrancers, if such I may call them, were in Henry II's time the important controllers of the revenue department which they became afterwards. The early rolls of the reign of Henry III indicate that their work was to note the exception rather than to record the rule. But it is evident that they cannot have been appointed originally at the beginning of Henry III's reign, and yet it is officially stated that their memoranda rolls begin with his first year.[1] Now there is hardly a year in the history of England in which it was less likely for a new administrative arrangement to be set up. Almost eleven months of it were occupied by civil war; the king was a child, and his supporters had all their powers engaged in the task of holding the throne for him. It is inconceivable that between October 1216 and

[1] Twentieth Report of the Deputy-Keeper of the Public Records (1859), pp. 41, 62; S. R. Scargill-Bird, Guide to the various Classes of Documents preserved in the Public Record Office (3rd ed., 1908), pp. 159 f. I am bound to add that I have not been able to find any of these rolls in the Office earlier than the 2nd year of Henry III. I do not understand the statement made in the Appendix to the General Report of his Majesty's Commission on the Public Records (1837), p. 196, that memoranda rolls of the lord treasurer's remembrancer exist for the 1st and 10th years of John.

Michaelmas 1217 Henry's ministers should have established a new system of financial control, which after all in the beginning did not amount to very much. More than this, fragments are preserved of a nature analogous to the contents of the remembrancers' rolls of a date prior to the reign of John,[1] and one of them appears to belong to the early years of Henry II. If this be so, there can be no *a priori* objection to our tracing their origin to the two confidential officers mentioned in the Dialogue. The only difficulty is that no one has been discovered who succeeded Thomas Brown. I am not sure that a closer study of the pipe rolls may not lead to a probable conjecture. But I would point out that the pipe rolls say nothing about the services performed by Thomas Brown; they only tell us what wages he received and what lands he held. Did we not possess the statement in the Dialogue we should have never known that he held a responsible place at the Exchequer.

These grants of land remind me to say a few words as to the manner in which the various officers of the Exchequer were paid. I have mentioned the daily wages of some of them and the perquisites recorded in the Establishment of the King's Household. But these were not the only emoluments which they received. To speak generally it would

---

[1] They are preserved among the Miscellanea of the Exchequer.

appear that the great officers of state held lands in fee attached to their offices, and their deputies held lands in serjeanty.[1] The officers of the assay likewise held lands in serjeanty.[2] The clerks were rewarded by ecclesiastical benefices. Thus Richard the son of Nigel, the treasurer, was archdeacon, canon, and dean before he was made bishop of London in 1189. Church preferment was indeed throughout the middle ages the usual way of paying civil servants who were in orders. But they also were holders of land. This is shown in a remarkable way in the case of several writers (*scribae*) under Henry I. As they were writers we may assume them to have been clergymen, and their duties were analogous to those of the modern civil service clerk. One of them, Gisulf, had a house at Winchester and held land in Cornwall early in the reign. Another, Bernard, who was of English origin, had five pieces of property in Cornwall and one in Surrey :[3] he succeeded to Gisulf's house at Winchester, which, I take it, was an official residence ;[4] it had previously belonged to Anselm the clerk. Bernard also succeeded to land

---

1 See Round, The King's Serjeants, pp. 47 f.

2 Introduction to the Dialogus, pp. 22 f. For the weigher's serjeanty see Mr. Round's paper on The Weigher of the Exchequer, in the English Historical Review, xxvi (1911) 724-727.

3 See Mr. Round's paper on Bernard the King's Scribe, ibid. xiv., 417 ff.

4 Ibid., p. 422 : cf. Liber Winton., p. 555.

formerly held by Gisulf in Cornwall.[1] Besides these properties he had inherited land, but the particular point to which I would call attention is not that these writers were men of substance but that their official position furnished them with houses and lands. Bernard had a squire in attendance.[2]

The chamberlain's clerk too is found to be a man of property. Thurstin, who was clerk to William of Pont de l'Arche, was granted lands by Henry I at Farringdon in Hampshire and at Bosham in Sussex; he also received licence to keep hounds for taking hares and foxes; and he had houses at Winchester. Under Henry II he rose to be sheriff of Hampshire, an office in which he was succeeded by his son Richard. That Richard was one of the sheriffs deprived after the inquest of sheriffs in 1170 shows that it was not only the local magnates who were deemed to have given cause for complaint.[3] Even the serjeants of the king's chapel held land, though we cannot prove that their holding was connected with their employment. Two of them, Buistard and Curteis, who witness a deed in a chartulary of Merton priory,[4] appear in the roll of 1130 as holders of a hide in Buckinghamshire[5] and of five hides in Warwickshire.[6]

---

1 Round, ubi supra, p. 418.

2 Ibid., p. 420.

3 See for all this Mr. Round's paper on The Rise of the Pophams, in The Ancestor, vii (1903) 59–63.

4 Round, in the English Historical Review, xiv. p. 423.

5 Roll of 31 Henry I, p. 102.

6 Ibid., pp. 107, 108.

Besides these emoluments the officers of the Exchequer enjoyed a number of privileges and exemptions. They could not be impleaded during the time of session; they were protected from insult; they paid nothing by way of customs.[1] What was far more important, they were free from all the great land taxes. When the itinerant justices imposed a common assize [2] on the hides of the county, the lands of those who held office at the Exchequer—not merely their demesne but all their fiefs—were exempt. They were also free from the fine charged upon the hundred for murder where the criminal was not discovered (*murdrum*): they paid no Danegeld [3] and no scutage.[4] The *perdonae* or discharges entered on their account on the rolls are of remarkable interest, because from them it is possible to identify the lands held by each officer according to the number of hides which he possessed in each hundred (for the *murdrum*) and each county (for Danegeld), and by the computation of their knight's fees (for scutage). Bishop Richard tells us that he had heard from his father Nigel that the exemption was for a time withdrawn under Henry I, but that the king afterwards decided that the loss of revenue involved by it was small in consideration

[1] Dialogus i. 8 p. 197.

[2] This is sometimes the *donum comitatus*, sometimes an assessment distributed over the county in commutation for amercements and other defaults. See the Notes to the Dialogus, p. 190.

[3] Danegeld was not levied after the 8th year of Henry II, but bishop Richard could not know that it would not be again imposed.

[4] Dialogus i. 8 p. 198.

of the great burthen[1] of office, and issued a writ declaring those who sat at the Exchequer for ever free from these taxes. Hence the discharges were constantly entered *per breve regis*, although there was in fact no special writ issued in each case.[2]

To conclude this part of our subject, the general impression which we derive from the description given of the board of Exchequer is that, while it retained its character as a meeting of the great officers of the king's Court, yet this theory was already breaking down under the stress of a more fully organized system of administration. The chancellor, the constable, and the keeper of the seal would probably not be seen there. The clerks or as we should say, the permanent officials, take their place. They were better versed in the details of finance than their chiefs, and there was no reason why these should attend unless they were called in to act in a judicial capacity, when difficult points arose for settlement. Thus insensibly the theory of a royal Court was changed into the reality of a committee of skilled officials, reinforced by the king's personal representatives, the remembrancers, who supervised the rendering and the audit of the sheriffs' accounts.

---

[1] I venture to read *oneris* in place of *honoris* in the Dialogus, i. 8 p. 200.

[2] Ibid., pp. 199 f.

VI

THE SHERIFF'S ACCOUNT

THE person who rendered his account at the Exchequer I call for convenience the sheriff, because his account comprises by far the greater part of what is entered on the great roll of the year known as the pipe roll. But the sheriffs were not the only accountants, to use the technical expression, at the Exchequer. Besides them there were the stewards and bailiffs of honours, the bailiffs and reeves of towns. There were guardians (*custodes*) of the temporalities of vacant bishoprics and abbacies, and there were guardians of escheated baronies and other fiefs. Guilds of craftsmen too paid their yearly licence duty. Hence bishop Richard is careful to specify ' the sheriff or guardian or whatever person sits at the account '.[1] It may however be presumed, even when it is not stated, that the sheriff acted on behalf of most of the smaller people from whom an account was due.

The mode of payment differed according as it was a normal yearly render or was something out of the ordinary course. In the latter case, when for instance the temporalities of a see were seized into the king's hand, the accountant was merely

[1] Dialogus, i. 5 p. 181; cf. ii. 27 p. 245; Inquest of Sheriffs, 1170, in Stubbs's Select Charters, p. 148.

the agent; he had to account in detail for every penny which he received from the estates. Sometimes the county itself was held in wardship (*in custodia*). But normally the sheriff or bailiff, as the rent-collector of the king's manors within his bailiwick, did not pay into the Treasury the rents as he received them: he paid instead a composition or lump sum; in other words, he farmed the manors. The amount for which he was responsible is called the sheriff's farm. It is common to speak as though this farm included all the royal rights in the county; and this is so far correct that there are a few sources of revenue, such as the proceeds of the local courts, independent of the king's manors which made part of the farm. But they formed a very small element in it, and in the interest of clearness may be best disregarded. The sheriff received many other things, the receipts for encroachments, the profits of the royal justice, and the like; he collected great levies, Danegeld, scutage, and aids: for all these he must render account, but he accounts for each item separately; they are no part of his farm.

It is important to bear in mind this distinction between the farm and the account as a whole, and the limitation of the primary charge on the roll. It was a matter between the sheriff and the crown, and no question arose as to the way in which he exacted from the tenants the sums for which he paid his composition. Only on a special occasion did Henry II go behind the accounts presented at the Exchequer. This was in 1170 when he returned to England after an absence of four years. Then by the Inquest of Sheriffs he ordered a strict examination not of the monies due to the crown but of the actual sums which the sheriffs, bailiffs, holders of franchises, and holders of other bailiwicks in wardship had received since the king's departure from England.[1] But ordinarily the sheriff was charged with his farm, and no further questions were asked on this head.

The amount of the farm may be stated as the yearly value of the king's manors in the shire or other bailiwick less the costs of collection. That however the profit earned by the sheriff was considerably in excess of this margin may be inferred from the heavy sums which were paid by him for obtaining his office.[2] But that matter does not concern us here. All we have to consider is the amount for which he was charged at the Exchequer, and for this I confine myself to the evidence which we possess for the reign of Henry II. The single roll which is preserved from the time of his grandfather is an invaluable record

[1] Inquest of Sheriffs, i–iv. pp. 148 f. Mr. Round has commented on the importance of clause iii. in The Commune of London, pp. 128 f.

[2] The most famous instance is the offer by archbishop Geoffrey of York in 1194 of £2000 and a yearly rent of 100 marks for the shrievalty of Yorkshire: Roger Howden, Chronica, iii. 241. The £2000 however were still unpaid in 1200: ibid. iv. 140.

of the financial procedure of 1130, but it has a number of membranes missing and moreover it is isolated. It is only from a series of rolls that we can learn what was the regular payment required; and for such a series we have to wait until the second year of Henry II.

Before however speaking of these rolls in detail, I must explain that in the twelfth century they never mention the amount of the farm. In Normandy the earliest known roll of the Exchequer, belonging to the year 1180,[1] introduces each section by a definite statement of the total amount due; but this convenient practice was not adopted in England until William of Ely became treasurer in the eighth year of Richard I. Down to that time the sum was not disclosed at the board of Exchequer, and was only produced after the sheriff had accounted for his outgoings. Alexander Swerford thought that it was kept secret *ut ignorarent vicecomites super quo deberent respondere*.[2] But in fact the sheriff was summoned at Easter to pay in a definite sum of money, which was the half of his farm;[3] and the reason why the amount was not inserted in the roll until the close of the Michaelmas audit was in order that there should be no risk of having to correct and erase the figures if any

[1] Printed by Stapleton, Magni Rotuli Scaccarii Normanniae, i (1840). A roll of 1176 is cited in that volume on p. 236, but it is not preserved.

[2] Red Book p. 659.

[3] Dialogus ii. 2 p. 213.

mistake was made in reckoning up the deductions.[1] Thus until the end of the twelfth century the gross amount of the farm was never entered; but only the balance between the sums paid in by the sheriff added to his outgoings, and the gross amount which was recorded on the *rotulus exactorius* or tax roll in the hands of the treasurer. This roll has not been preserved. If, as we may gather, it was merely a schedule of the totals payable from the several counties, boroughs, honours, and other peculiar bailiwicks and wardships,[2] it ran to no great length, and may well have been comprised in a single membrane. When it came to be the practice to enter the total on the pipe roll, it was unnecessary that the tax roll should be preserved, and we may in this way explain its disappearance.

The form in which the account of the farm is drawn up, though it is in fact very simple, is apt to cause difficulty to those who begin the study of the pipe rolls. If we were to prepare such an account, we should set down first the gross sum demanded, then deduct from it the total amount which the sheriff has paid out of pocket, and finally charge him with the balance. The pipe roll inverts the process: it opens by a statement of what is paid or due, that is the balance; then goes

---

1 ii. 27 p. 246.

2 Mr. G. J. Turner thinks that it was more detailed: see his valuable paper on the Sheriff's Farm, in the Transactions of the Royal Historical Society, New Series, xii (1898) 131.

on to add to this the list of outgoings ; but leaves you to find out the total by yourself. Of course it is only a difference of method, but it leads to some results which are liable to be misunderstood. For example, when, as is very frequently the case, the sheriff's account ends with the words 'And he owes' so much, one might infer that he was either remiss in collecting the monies for which he was responsible or else that he had difficulty in meeting the demands made upon him. Neither inference is necessary. The sheriff was bound, just as a modern man of business is bound, to keep a balance. Not only were there regular outgoings which might have to be paid before any new money came in, but also the sheriff was liable to receive at any time royal orders for expenditure of various kinds and often of very large amount. Consequently he had to arrange not to pay in so much of his farm as would leave him without means for meeting whatever calls were made upon him. When, on the other hand, as sometimes happens, the roll states that 'he has a surplus', one naturally thinks that the particular sheriff has been exceptionally provident ; but the words imply exactly the reverse. The sheriff has a surplus because he has paid in so much into the Treasury that he has not left himself enough to meet the king's occasional demands. These he pays out of his own pocket, and the account has in fact a deficit which will have to be made good in the next financial year. The explanation of this apparent paradox is that, as I have tried to show, the sheriff's account is rendered in terms of negatives. The items are all added together in order that they may be finally subtracted from the farm. Every sum we add is a fresh deduction from the amount which the sheriff has to pay. If the account ends with a debit balance, it means that the sheriff has some money in hand which he will pay in the following year: if it ends with a surplus, the sheriff will add this to his deductions in the next account.

The system of the farm of the shire was fully established under Henry I, and it was maintained, possibly with interruptions, in the reign of Stephen.[1] The pipe roll of the second year of Henry II proves that the Exchequer was at work in the last years of his predecessor.[2] But there is no question that the amount of loss to the Treasury in consequence of the devastation of a large part of the country was enormous;[3] and the revenue was diminished not only by this cause but also by the reckless grants of land made to their supporters by the rival

[1] See Round, Geoffrey de Mandeville, 1892, pp. 92, 142, 154, for evidence as to 1141. The Exchequer buildings at Westminster were in need of repair when Henry II came to the throne: see the Roll of his second year, p. 4 in two places.

[2] See Turner, ubi supra, pp. 127 f.

[3] Dialogus i. 8 p. 199. See the figures collected by Mr. H. W. C. Davis, The Anarchy of Stephen's Reign, in the English Historical Review, xix (1903) 634, 639 f.

claimants to the throne.[1] The king's income suffered profoundly, but the farm for which the sheriff was accountable remained in principle unaffected.[2] If there was waste which the sheriff made good, he paid so much 'for the restoration of the manors' and deducted the amount from his farm. The same was the case with regard to the crown lands which had been alienated, the *terrae datae* as they are termed. The sheriff gives in his account a list of lands granted by the king with their annual value in order that he may be allowed for them, in other words that his charge may be reduced by this amount. Substantially the same list may appear from year to year: lands granted in the sixth year of Henry II will be repeated as late as the twenty-second, or later. They are a permanent loss to the farm;—how great a loss, may be seen from a calculation made by Dr. Parow[3] that in the sixteenth year the farms of the counties amounted to just under £10,000 blank, from

---

1 Cf. Round, pp. 99, 275.

2 For example, in the 22nd year of Henry II the sheriff of Gloucestershire paid in to the Exchequer £84 0s. 2d. To this has to be added £50 for the farm of the borough of Gloucester, for which its reeve accounted separately (as he had done since Easter 1165, Roll of 11 Henry II, p. 12), but the sum had to appear in the sheriff's account too because it was separated after the farm was settled. The sheriff was forgiven his balance of £13 14s. 8d. Hence for a farm of £372 13s. 6d. only £134 0s. 2d. reached the Exchequer. The rest was made up out of *terrae datae* and fixed or casual outgoings.

3 Compotus Vicecomitis, p. 27.

which *terrae datae* of the value of £3663 15s. 7d. had to be deducted. The farm was therefore on an average diminished by nearly 35 per cent. The farms of honours and towns were almost exactly £4000 blank, but these had not been so largely reduced by grants of land; the loss on them was not much more than £500. It might seem to us simpler, supposing lands of the value of £50 to have been alienated, to change a farm of £400 to £350. But this would not have worked in practice, for it was always possible that some of the lands might escheat to the crown through failure of heirs, and in such cases, unless they were placed specially *in custodia,* they passed back into the farm.[1]

The amount of the farm was a definite sum fixed at the Exchequer before the summonses to the Easter sessions were sent out. At the beginning of Henry II's reign it varied slightly from year to year in consequence of the difficulty of ascertaining exactly to how much the king was entitled after a period of disorganization. By the sixth year they settle down to a normal amount from which they rarely differ unless a definite alteration was arbitrarily made. When the farms had become practically fixed, it was not uncommon to make an addition to them, as when fresh land was brought under tillage, under a separate designation:

[1] See an example in Turner, ubi supra, pp. 136 f.

either the new charge was described as 'of increment' (*de cremento*); or else the farm was stated to be so much blank and so much by tale, the amount payable by tale being the additional levy. Sometimes the payment for the increment was not charged in money but took the form of the render of a certain number of hawks.[1]

The farm, as I have said, formed only a part of the account for which the sheriff was charged at the Exchequer. The other items, which I shall mention later, do not admit of precise statement, because they were derived from varying sources of revenue; but it has been estimated that, in a year in which there was no Danegeld or scutage or aid, they might amount to a sum not far short, perhaps nine-tenths, of the net farms after deduction of the *terrae datae*.[2] Giraldus Cambrensis is unexpectedly near the truth in the account he gives of the history of the revenue in the twelfth century. After repeating the figment, for which he vouches the authority of Domesday Book, that at the time of the Norman Conquest the revenue amounted to 60,000 marks, he says

[3] By the time of king Henry II, so much land had been

[1] Thus in the Roll of 23 Henry II, p. 156.

[2] See Parow, pp. 48 f.

[3] Angliae, regum Anglorum tempore et etiam penultimi Edwardi Westmonasteriensis diebus, annui fiscales redditus, sicut [in] rotulo Wintoniae reperitur, ad sexaginta millium marcarum summam implebant; tempore vero regis Henrici secundi, tot terris

granted to knights both by king Stephen and himself, by reason of the almost constant wars waged first between them and afterwards against France, that the returns of the Treasury were found hardly to amount to 12,000 marks a year. One may therefore ask, or marvel in silence, how it was that king Henry II and his sons, in spite of their many wars, abounded so much in treasure. The reason is this, that as they had less in rents they took care to make up the total by occasional incomings and relied more on accessory than on the principal sources of revenue.

Before entering upon the form in which the account was enrolled, I will give a summary of what is said in the Dialogue about the procedure which regulated the mode of its render. This was made in three stages, which were distinguished from the thirteenth century onwards as the 'profer', the 'view of the account', and the 'summ'.[1] In the first stage, both at Easter and Michaelmas, the sheriff paid in money. The 'view' took place at Easter, when he made his *vere dictum*

---

interim militibus tam a rege Stephano prius, quam ab ipso postmodum, tum propter werras primum inter ipsos postmodum erga Franciam fere continuas, large utrimque datis, vix annui duodecim millium marcarum redditus fiscales sunt inventi. Quaeri ergo potest ab aliquo, vel tacitum etiam quempiam movere, qualiter rex Henricus secundus et eius filii tot inter werras tantis thesauris abundabant. Ad quae ratio reddi poterit, quia, quod minus habebant in redditibus, totum in accidentibus, plus in accessoriis quam principalibus confidentes, supplere curabant: De Principis Instructione, ed. G. F. Warner, 1891, iii. 30 p. 316 (Opera, viii).

[1] Madox xxiii. 2 p. 644.

or verbal declaration as to what allowances and discharges were due to him, without producing the 'warrant' in the shape of writs and quittances.[1] The 'summ' or completion of the account was made at Michaelmas, when full evidence of all particulars had to be furnished and was recorded on the roll.

[2] In order that the Exchequer may be held there are summonses issued. For the persons who must attend are first summoned by a writ under the king's seal to a place named: unless they receive a summons they need not attend. There are two classes of persons at the exchequer: first, the barons who sit and judge either by virtue of their office or by the king's order; secondly, the sheriffs and other persons who pay and are judged, being chargeable some with voluntary offerings, some with compulsory payments. Now on account of the number of persons who have to be summoned from all the counties, it is necessary to state precisely in each writ how much is to be paid at the forthcoming term and for what cause. Suppose a sheriff when making his account to be called upon for any matter relating to any debtor in his county who has not been mentioned in his summons, he is not bound to answer; he is excused because there has been no summons for the particular matter. The object of the summonses is that the Treasury may get possession of the royal farms and of monies owing to it in various

---

[1] Madox xxiii. 2 pp. 646 f.; Notes to the Dialogus p. 208.

[2] Dialogus ii. 1 pp. 210 f. An excellent paraphrase of the following passages is given by Mr. Melville M. Bigelow in his History of Procedure in England, 1880, pp. 114–122. I regret that I had not the advantage of reading this book until my lectures were written.

ways. There are however some payments which must be made through the sheriff even though they be not mentioned in the summons: these are not the settled or fixed payments but casual sources of revenue, as will be explained hereafter.

When the Exchequer of the term at which the summonses are made is closed, the treasurer's clerks take out the sums due to the king county by county from the great roll of that year, and record them on shorter rolls with a note of the reason for each claim. Then the barons (*maiores*) retire for consultation and settle how much is to be summoned from each county and from each debtor in it,[1] having regard to the quality of the person and of the business or cause for which he is bounden to the king. The authoritative roll of the year, from which these claims are extracted, is held by the treasurer or his clerk for reference in order that there may not by any chance be an error in making the extracts. Meanwhile another clerk carefully takes down what they have settled in their extracts, concerning which the summons is in the following terms:

> Henry king of the English to such or such a sheriff greeting. See as you love yourself and all that you have that you be at the Exchequer at such a place on the morrow of Michaelmas, or the morrow of the close of Easter, and have there with you whatsoever you owe of the old farm [that is, the arrears of last year] or of the new, and specifically the debts following: from such a one ten marks for this cause,

and so forth. All the debts are set out with their causes which are contained in the great roll of the year. Then all the smaller rolls of the itinerant judges are brought forward, and whatever falls due to the king in each county

[1] Not surely 'every taxpayer', as Mr. Bigelow takes it, p. 118: the *debitores* are the sheriffs, bailiffs, guardians, and the like.

through their labour and industry is extracted from them.[1] And when these have been settled by the great officers, they are inserted in the summonses; and when the whole is arranged in order, the summons is completed as follows:

> And you shall have all these things with you in monies, tallies, writs, and quittances, or they will be taken from your farm. Witness such or such a person, at such a place, at the Exchequer.

The sheriff is thus to bring first cash, secondly tallies for what he has already paid at Easter, thirdly writs for payments out of pocket authorized by writ, and fourthly quittances for like payments not so authorized because admitted as customary. If he fails to bring them, they will be 'taken out of' his farm; that is to say, he will not be allowed to deduct them (i.e. the sums mentioned in the writs and quittances) from his farm: and if he does not pay in all the monies which he ought to have collected from other sources, he will be charged first with them, and what he has brought with him in order to satisfy his farm will be correspondingly reduced.

[2] Moreover, by a modern ordinance, that is after the time of king Henry I, the following was added in summonses:

> if perchance you are summoned for the debt of any man who has no land or chattels in your bailiwick, and you know in whose bailiwick or county he has them, you shall signify the same by your writ to that sheriff or bailiff, by the hand of your messenger who shall deliver your writ to him in the county court, if possible, or in the presence of several persons.

---

[1] Cf. Dialogus ii. 2 p. 215. [2] ii. 1 p. 211.

This additional clause was necessitated by some people's vexatious subterfuges. For knowing the times when the summonses were sent out, before the summons for their debt reached the county, they would empty their barns and disperse their goods whither they would or pack them off to safe places, and then sit at home destitute, awaiting in security the arrival of the sheriff and the other officials. So for a long time by this device the authority of the king's writ was mocked at. For this reason the clause given above was inserted in the summonses, and there was no room left for evasion to save the debtor from making satisfaction unless he was excused by extreme poverty. But when it became clear to all sheriffs and debtors that by this means an end could be put to proceedings of this sort, it was no longer necessary to add the clause given above, and it is not now inserted; but the mode of coercion of debtors, whithersoever they have withdrawn themselves, is maintained by the sheriffs and upheld as though established by a perpetual law.

[1] The Exchequer is held twice in the year, and each time summonses are issued for it. At the Easter term there are taken from the sheriffs not accounts but views of accounts; so that hardly any of the business is committed to writing,[2] but the whole is reserved for the next term, so that it may be then entered item by item in order in the great roll of the year. But certain particulars to be borne in mind (*memoranda*) which often arise are then written down separately by the treasurer's clerk, so that when the Exchequer of that term is closed the barons may decide about them: unless they were recorded they

[1] ii. 2 pp. 212 ff.

[2] That is, apparently, as a final record. It seems from what follows that the memoranda contained entries of debts remaining in arrear. Under Richard I the account of the Easter 'view' is found attached as a schedule to the pipe roll: see Madox xxiii. 2 p. 646 *w*.

would not easily occur to the memory on account of their great number. Moreover, [a note is kept of] whatsoever a sheriff has paid into the Treasury of his farm, and then if he has satisfied [the board], in the same line is written 'And he is quit:' if not, the amount owing is set down distinctly in a lower line, so that it may be known how much of the sum of that term is lacking and that he may forthwith make satisfaction according to the judgement of the president. For every sheriff is bound to pay at that term one half of the farm arising for the year from his county.

In these summonses the language does not vary except so far as concerns the date and place, supposing for instance that the barons decide to hold the Easter Exchequer at one place and the Michaelmas Exchequer at another. But although the same terms are preserved in both summonses, there is a difference in the note of the debts extracted [from the memoranda]. For in the summons made against Easter term, because the year is taken to begin then,[1] the phrase is simply, 'From such a one you shall have £10,' and from this summons he shall not be absolved except by then paying or making satisfaction[2] for £10. But when there comes to be made the summons for Michaelmas term, at which the year is closed and terminated, and the roll of the year is made, there will be added to the £10 aforesaid another £10 or more, as shall seem good to the barons, and the words will be 'From such a one you shall have £20'. But suppose the accountant has paid £10 of this sum at the Easter term, he will now pay £10 in cash and produce a tally for the £10 already paid, and will thus be absolved from his

---

[1] The summonses for Easter were settled immediately after the close of the Michaelmas Exchequer, when the financial year began: see above, p. 139.

[2] That is, by means of tallies or writs of allowance or discharge.

summons. For the terms of the summons are: 'All these you shall have in money and writs and tallies.'

When a summons has been written, if while it is being corrected a mistake is found, it must not be cancelled by means of a line drawn below nor erased, because the writing is patent [and therefore liable to being tampered with]: the words written in error must be completely obliterated, so that nothing of the writing can be read. No doubt the sheriff may alter the writ after he has received it, because the barons keep no copy;[1] but it would be very dangerous to do so, because all the debts concerning which summonses are issued are diligently recorded elsewhere. Moreover, for greater security, the archdeacon of Poitiers [for a time] caused copies to be made of all summonses and allowed no writs to be sent out before copies of them were made and carefully corrected. So, when the sheriff came to account and the chancellor's clerk read the summons, the archdeacon's clerk[2] kept his eye on the copy and watched lest he deviated from it. But after a time, when the number of debtors increased immensely, so that the length of one skin would hardly suffice to contain [the writs for] a single summons, the practice was given up and the officers were satisfied with the original summons alone, as formerly.

---

[1] Enrolment of the writs of summons had therefore not begun; but the memoranda already mentioned must have served as a check upon fraudulent alteration of the summonses.

[2] In the account of the session of the Exchequer (above, p. 116) it is said that the archdeacon's colleague Thomas Brown had a writer there, but there is no mention of the archdeacon's clerk. Probably one of the two statements is due to inadvertence: there was a remembrancer's clerk in the Exchequer, and bishop Richard accidentally attached him to different remembrancers.

The inconvenience caused by the multitude of entries of debts that could never be recovered, because the debtor was dead or for other reasons, was perceived in the 28th year of Henry II when they were removed from the account of the shire and placed by themselves in a separate pipe prefixed to the roll.[1]

Bishop Richard has then a digression on the eminent success of Henry II in establishing peace. After the great rebellion of his wife and sons in 1173–4, he treated the conquered with unheard-of mercy: very few suffered loss of their goods, and none of their life or condition.

[2] Therefore, when peace was restored, after the shipwrecked state of the kingdom, the king took steps to renew again the times of old. He chose discreet men and divided the kingdom into six parts,[3] so that the itinerant justices (*iudices errantes*), as we call them, should pass through it and re-establish the rights of which the people had been deprived. They made their authority felt in every county and administered justice to those who

---

[1] When the form of the account was remodelled by the Provisions made in the Exchequer in the 12th year of Edward I (Statutes of the Realm i. 69) a separate roll was made *de firmis mortuis et debitis de quibus non est spes*. These Provisions came to be described erroneously as the Statute of Rutland (meaning Rhuddlan) and were assigned to the 10th year. They are enrolled on the close roll of 12 Edward I m. 7 dors. (Calendar of Close Rolls, 1279–1288, pp. 294 ff.). The roll of 'dead farms' was known as the Exannual Roll.

[2] Dialogus ii. 2 pp. 215 f.

[3] By the assize of Northampton, 1176.

thought themselves wronged, thus saving both trouble and expense to the poor. In these visitations divers crimes were punished in divers ways in consideration of the nature of the offence ; so that some received punishment in their body, and others in their money. Now the money penalties are carefully noted in the rolls of the itinerant justices,[1] and, when the Exchequer sits, they are delivered to the treasurer in the sight of all. But the judges have to be careful to send in to the treasurer accurate rolls properly arranged in order ; for after they have been handed in it is not lawful even for the judges themselves to change a jot, not though all the judges agree therein. If a mistake occurs, it is their own fault, because there are times granted them for correction and they know the appointed law : the amount stated will be required of the debtors, if they are condemned to this amount, or from the judges themselves. Suppose they have described on the roll a man as condemned to the payment of a score, and, when the voucher is handed in to the treasurer, they remember that he was only bound in ten, the judges themselves shall make satisfaction for the residue ; for they cannot recall that which they have written and corrected with deliberation after it has once been handed in.

The debts contained in the rolls handed in the treasurer causes to be diligently and distinctly recorded in the great roll, county by county, likewise with the causes, with a note of the names of the judges, so that in this way the sums exacted may be distinguished. Of these matters the summonses should be drawn up thus : 'Of the pleas of such and such persons, from such a one so much and

[1] These are the eyre rolls from which in later times estreats (that is, extracts) were sent in to the Exchequer to be enrolled on the memoranda roll of the lord treasurer's remembrancer.

from such a one so much,' according as the barons have beforehand settled the debts.

[1] All sheriffs and bailiffs to whom summonses are addressed are bound by the authority of the king's writ, to appear at the time and place appointed and to satisfy their debts. Supposing that he is in default in paying the debts recited in the writ, the sums due from other people will be taken from his farm, and he will have to make up his farm from his own chattels and from the rents of his estates, and in the meanwhile, if the barons so determine, he will be placed in a sure place under free custody. When therefore the sheriff receives the summons, he must come on the appointed day and show himself to the president, if he happen to attend, or in his absence to the treasurer. Then, having saluted the barons, he is free for the day, but must return on the morrow and each day following. If perchance he does not come nor send a lawful excuse, on the first day he is condemned to the king in 100 shillings of silver for each county [of which he is sheriff];[2] on the second, in ten pounds of silver; on the third, as we have heard from those who were before us, all the goods that he possesses will be at the king's good pleasure; and on the fourth, since he is now proved to have contemned the king's majesty, he will be at his mercy not only in his goods but his own person. Some however are of opinion that a money penalty suffices for the whole amount, namely 100 shillings for each day. I do not

---

[1] Dialogus ii. 3 p. 216.

[2] Many counties were held in pairs by a single sheriff, as Cambridgeshire and Huntingdonshire are held to this day. Thus the counties of Buckingham and Bedford, Warwick and Leicester, Nottingham and Derby, Essex and Hertford, and Norfolk and Suffolk, Dorset and Somerset, had each a sheriff in common; but in the last case the accounts were sometimes rendered separately. See Turner, ubi supra, pp. 142–148.

contest the statement, provided that the king, against whom the offence is committed, approves. For it is quite probable that he may accept this manner of punishment, for his singular grace is slow to inflict punishment and swift to reward. The writ says that if the sheriff is in default in paying the sums mentioned in it, they shall be taken from his farm. But suppose he has expended the whole of it by king's writs or in works or otherwise, what then? In that case he will be detained on his own security in such place as the barons may determine, until he has made satisfaction for these debts as he had to do for the farm.

In the following statement which deals with the procedure allowed when the sheriff was unable to carry out his duties at the Exchequer in person, a distinction is drawn between what was permitted when he paid in or satisfied the debt due from him, or in the later phrase when he made his 'profer',[1] and what was required when he came to account. In the second case the rules were much more strict than in the first.[2]

[3] If the sheriff is detained by sickness, he may send the money which he has collected by his servants accompanied by a letter of excuse. One or both of his messengers must be a knight or a layman connected with him by blood or otherwise. Clergymen alone must not be charged with the duty, because if they misbehave it is not proper to imprison them for money or accounts. A valid excuse frees the sheriff from the penalties for non-attendance at

[1] See Madox xxiii. 2 pp. 644 ff.

[2] See ibid., xxiii. 5 pp. 658 ff.; Notes to the Dialogus, p. 214.

[3] Dialogus ii. 4 pp. 218 ff.

payment. On the other hand, for the completion of his account no one is admitted except[1] his eldest son, not even his general proctor, even though he have his writ authorizing him to act for him. Only by the king's order or, in his absence, by that of the president can he substitute another to fulfil his account; but if he is employed on other business laid upon him by the king, he may at the Exchequer in person nominate some one there present to carry out his duties for him. The writ of the king or president or of the sheriff excusing himself shall be kept in the marshal's forel. If the sheriff is called abroad by the king or has licence to go abroad on private business, he must first approach the president and delegate his functions by word of mouth to some lawful man. In such a case he need send no writ or excuse his absence. If a sheriff is excused for illness, when his account comes to be written for the roll of the year, it will be said, 'William sheriff of London, Robert his son for him, renders account for the farm of London.' But if another is substituted for him by the king's order, or if he himself by word of mouth has designated any one to the president in his place, the record must be written throughout as though he had attended at the account in person. Other excuses for absence are admitted, such as the death of the sheriff's eldest son or the serious illness of his wife, or compulsory attendance on his liege lord in a lawsuit; again, if the lord wishes to make his will or if the sheriff has to make arrangements for his lord's funeral, or for that of his own wife or son, he may claim to be excused.

Before he appears to make account he must pay what is required of him and his payment must be assayed.

---

[1] The reading *nisi* in the Black Book appears to be supported by the example given below: the Oxford edition has *nec*.

This is the preliminary business at the Treasury of Receipt.

[1] Then he takes his seat at the Exchequer, and all the other sheriffs are excluded. Before this he sends round notice by means of a cryer to all persons whom it may concern [2] on what day he is to attend. Then at the appointed time the treasurer calls upon him to render his account and asks him whether the allowances are the same as in the preceding year. If this is the case, the treasurer's writer copies out the roll of the preceding year in regard to these allowances.

At this point bishop Richard leaves the subject of the account which he had in fact dealt with in an earlier chapter and to which he reverts near the end of his book.[3] I have given this long extract—long, though I have very much abridged it—because it gives a good example of the writer's lucidity and care for details. But the manner in which the account was completed will be best explained in connexion with the form it took upon the roll.

---

[1] Dialogus i. 4 p. 220.

[2] See the Notes to the Dialogus, p. 215.

[3] Dialogus ii. 27 p. 246.

VII

THE GREAT ROLL OF THE YEAR

THE account rendered by the sheriff at the Exchequer was recorded on the great roll of the year. In the Dialogue it is spoken of as the roll of the Treasury (*rotulus de thesauro* [1]), the roll of the year (*rotulus annalis* [2]), the great roll of the year,[3] or the great roll of accounts of the year (*magni annales compotorum rotuli* [4]). It consisted of a number of membranes, each of which was called a pipe,[5] because, as I presume, it naturally rolled up and looked like a cylinder or pipe. That this was the technical meaning of the word 'pipe' can be proved from the reign of Edward II;[6] *la pipe* was the single membrane containing the account of a single sheriff,[7] though this sometimes extended into two or more membranes separately headed.[8] By 1348 the combined roll is called *la*

---

[1] i. 5 p. 178.

[2] i. 7 p. 194; 11 p. 205; *annalis* simply, ii. 18 p. 240.

[3] ii. 1 p. 211.

[4] i. 14 p. 207.

[5] This is the official interpretation of the word, 'the "pipes" or membranes of the sheriff's normal county accounts': introduction to List of Foreign Accounts (Public Record Office, Lists and Indexes, xi), 1900; cf. sir J. H. Ramsay, in the English Historical Review, xxvi. (1911) 329 f.

[6] Red Book of the Exchequer, pp. 858, 860.

[7] Ibid., pp. 850, 874.

[8] See Ramsay, ubi supra, p. 330; and compare p. 749.

pipe, and at a date which I have not ascertained it becomes known as *magnus rotulus pipae*. But this belongs only to later usage. The pipe roll is a roll of pipes, just as a pine wood is a wood of pines; and any fanciful interpretation, such as that which traces the name to the resemblance of the bulky roll to a pipe or cask of wine, or to the pipe or channel through which the king drew his revenue, must be dismissed as unhistorical.

Each pipe consisted of two strips of sheepskin sewn together to form one length. Bishop Richard thinks that the material was chosen because it was difficult to make an erasure upon it without leaving a trace;[1] and this may have been one reason for its selection. But parchment (*pergamena*) meant any writing material made from skin, whether of sheep, goat, or calf; and sheep's skin is said to have been the most usual material, especially in Italy, after papyrus became unobtainable. So it is possible that the English clerks were merely using what naturally came to hand. The length of the double skin varied between 3 feet and 4 feet 8 inches. Its breadth is accurately described in the Dialogue as a span and a half, that is, between $13\frac{1}{2}$ and 14 inches.[2] When the pipes of all the sheriffs and other accountants—to use the official

---

[1] Dialogus i. 5 p. 187.

[2] Late in the thirteenth century the rolls are somewhat broader. This, I am informed, was due to the improvement in the breed of sheep.

phrase—were completed, they were filed at the head, and thus made up into the great roll of the year.[1] The order in which the separate pipes were stitched together was quite capricious, and probably no roll presents the counties in the same order.[2]

The roll was always cited as the roll of a given year of the king's reign. It is essential to understand exactly what this year means. The roll was made up in Michaelmas, and the regnal year is the year in which that Michaelmas fell.[3] The accounts it contains are the accounts of the twelve months preceding that Michaelmas. Hence the roll of a given regnal year may be concerned largely or even mainly with the accounts of the regnal year next preceding. Thus Richard I's reign is dated from his coronation on 3 September 1189: the roll was made up four weeks later, and hence almost the whole of this roll of the 1st year of Richard I deals with the accounts of the 35th year of Henry II. No roll for that 35th year ever

[1] This mode of filing distinguished the rolls of the Exchequer from those of the Chancery, which begin under John. The Chancery rolls are sewn continuously so as to make one single roll, and the membranes are numbered backwards from that lowest on the roll.

[2] See a table of the various arrangements of the accounts in 31 Henry I and 2–6 Henry II in the Introduction to the Study of the Pipe Rolls, p. 52.

[3] J. Hunter, preface to Magnus Rotulus Scaccarii, 31 Henry I, p. xv; Round, Studies on the Red Book of the Exchequer, p. 21.

existed, because it began on 19 December and therefore included no Michaelmas. This then is the rule: the roll of a given year is the roll of the Michaelmas which fell within that year.[1] It is worth while mentioning here that when a roll refers to the preceding year (*praeteritus annus*), the third year, the fourth year, and the like, the reckoning was always backwards until the reign of John, when *praeteritus annus* was alone allowed, and the years before that were cited by the Exchequer years of the king; so that in the third year of John the references were to the last year, then to the first year [of John], then to the tenth year [of Richard I].[2]

The earliest pipe roll preserved[3] is that of the thirty-first year of Henry I which was edited by Joseph Hunter in 1833. It was long believed to be that of the fifth year of Stephen and is regularly cited as such by Madox, but in a letter to lord Somers which he appended to his book he proved that it must belong to the reign of Henry I,[4] and

---

[1] A neglect of this rule has led to the misdating of a series of entries in the edition of the Red Book of the Exchequer, pp. 9–12, 70–184.

[2] Madox, Disceptatio epistolaris addressed to lord Somers, pp. 68 f., appended to the History of the Exchequer; Hunter, p. xi.

[3] In Henry III's time there were more than one. Swerford speaks of having inspected *paucos annales* of the reign: Red Book of the Exchequer, p. 5.

[4] Disceptatio epistolaris, pp. 70–75. He had previously expressed the same opinion in the preface to his Formu-

Hunter in the preface to his edition, which is a model of historical criticism, demonstrated that the year with which it dealt was the thirty-first year, ending at Michaelmas 1130. Then there is a gap and the regular series of rolls begins with that of the second year of Henry II.[1] A duplicate or counter-roll was made for the chancellor; and, though this set is defective, it serves to supply the few years in which the pipe roll is lost.

The form in which the roll was drawn up is concisely explained in the section of the Dialogue dealing with the treasurer's writer, or clerk of the pells;[2] its details are further elucidated in nine chapters of the second book.[3]

> The rolls are ruled from the top almost to the foot and on both sides with lines at a seemly distance from one another, and there are marked at the top of the roll the counties and bailiwicks concerning which account is rendered below. Then after a small space of three or four fingers' breadths is written in the middle of the line the name of the county to be first dealt with. Then at the beginning of the next line the name of the sheriff is inserted, with the words following, *Such or such a sheriff renders account for the farm of such or such a county.* Then a little further in the line is written, *In the Treasury*; but the sum is not added until the account is concluded.

---

lare Anglicanum (1702) § 6. Prynne in the appendix to Aurum Reginae, p. 5, assigned the roll to 18 Henry I.

[1] A summary of the roll of the first year is given by Swerford, pp. 648–658.

[2] i. 5 pp. 186 f.

[3] From the end of ii. 4 p. 220 to ii. 12 p. 234.

The reason for this I have already explained:[1] the exact figures could not be set down until all the deductions were made. Very often this entry is preceded by a record of a specific payment *de veteri firma*, that is for the arrears of the last year, or even *de tertio anno* or the year before that. These sums are reckoned by themselves and balanced with the 'old farm'; they do not affect the account of the farm of the current year.

> Then at the beginning of the next line is entered what has been expended from the farm of the county in alms and appointed tithes and in livery (*in liberatione*).

These are the 'settled' or fixed allowances for payments made by the sheriff out of pocket. The alms paid to the knights templars are a regular item. Most counties were charged with one mark, but a few with two.[2] The majority of the towns and honours which accounted separately paid nothing; but nine of them were charged with a mark each.[3] The other alms paid differ in different counties, and vary greatly in their amount. Sometimes they indicate a payment of one or more pennies a day: for instance, the

---

[1] Above, pp. 130 f.

[2] In the Roll of 23 Henry II Kent, London and Middlesex, Lincolnshire, Yorkshire, and Worcestershire each paid two marks; Essex and Hertfordshire 4 marks jointly; Norfolk and Suffolk together 3 marks. Rutland was not charged.

[3] These in the same Roll were Winchester, Southampton, Lincoln, Northampton, Meon, Bosham, Waltham, Higham [Ferrers], and the honour of Eye.

sheriff of Norfolk and Suffolk paid £4 11s. 3d. to the brethren of the hospital at Norwich, that is 3d. a day.[1] The tithes were paid to churches and religious houses, and as a rule it is not said on what property the tithe was assessed. Sometimes however this is stated: for instance,

In tithes appointed to the canons of Colchester 100s. for the tithes of Hatfield.[2]

The liveries are in part hardly distinguishable from alms. As is pointed out in the Dialogue, they fall into two classes:

[3] Some are for the needy, when from pure charity the king assigns a man a penny or two, or more, a day for food and raiment. Others are for servants, by way of wages: such are paid to household servants, musicians, wolf-catchers, and the like. Although the king may grant liveries of the former sort to any needy persons, by old custom they are given to those who have served in the Court and possess no property and who have become unable to work by reason of bodily infirmity.[4]

As examples of both kinds of bounty and of payments in fixed sums as well as by the day

---

[1] Roll of 23 Henry II, p. 124.

[2] Ibid., p. 144. A precise statement of the source of the tithe appears in the account of the forest of Wiltshire in the Roll of 3 Henry II, p. 79: *Henricus Esturmi reddit Compotum de .iiii.li. et .x.s. de Censu foreste de Sauernac. In thesauro .iiii.li. et .xii.d. Et in Decimis Constitutis Canonicis Sarisberie .ix.s. Et Quietus est.*

[3] ii. 6 p. 221.

[4] In the Oxford edition this last sentence is bracketed as a gloss: see the Notes, p. 216.

I may quote from the roll of the 23rd year of Henry II under Surrey: [1]

> And in appointed livery to the sick in the queen's hospital, 30s. 5d. And to John the almoner 30s. 5d. And to the same 6s. 8d. for clothes. And to Brichtmar the lame 5s. And to Roger son of Codulf 60s. 10d. And to John of the Chapel 60s. 10d. And to Suein the velterer [2] 30s. 5d.

Some charges in this class were really salaries to public officials. Thus the master of the king's yacht (*esnecca*) received a shilling a day, for which the tallies were made by the chamberlains.[3] Again, the sheriff of Kent regularly paid 20s. to the porter of the city of Canterbury, *quia facit iustitiam comitatus*,[4] because he was the public executioner. Down to modern times the rooms over the west gate of Canterbury were the prison, and we may still see there the cells and the various implements of duress pertaining to such a place. Sometimes payments from the county farm were made in respect of towns which kept a separate account. For example, the gatekeeper and watchman of Dover received £6 1s. 8d., or 4d. a day,[5] because the king had a special interest in securing the safety of one of his principal seaports.

---

[1] p. 192.

[2] The man who had charge of 'greyhounds': see Round, The King's Serjeants, p. 269.

[3] Dialogus i. 6 p. 193.

[4] Roll of 23 Henry II, p. 202.

[5] Ibid.

The description of the roll proceeds:

[1] After this, at the beginning of the next line, under the head of *terrae datae* are noted the grants which the king has made from his crown estates to churches or to those who serve them,[2] some blank, some by tale.

These grants of land were by no means only grants to churches. In treating of the sheriff's account as a whole I have pointed out the bearing of the entry.[3] The *terrae datae* were simply sums, as we should say, written off. The lands were alienated and the farm which the sheriff had to pay in to the Treasury was reduced by their amount. The distinction made between lands granted blank and those granted by tale was of great importance to the sheriff. To the grantee it made no difference at all: he held the lands and had nothing to pay. But the sheriff had to account for them at a different rate according to the mode of the grant. Bishop Richard explains the distinction as follows:

[4] When the king grants an estate together with the hundred court (*cum hundredo*) or the pleas which proceed from it, they call that estate granted him blank: but when he grants the estate simply and retains the hundred, by which the farm is said to be blanched (*dealbari*), it is called granted by tale.

---

[1] Dialogus i. 5 p. 186.

[2] *Qui eis militarunt.* The word *militare* has passed into the general sense of 'serving'. Cf. *Ricardi bonae memoriae Lond. episcopi, . . . qui quartus ante eum in ecclesia beati Pauli militavit*: John of Salisbury, Epist. xxxix.

[3] Above, pp. 134 f.

[4] Dialogus ii. 5 p. 220.

If the hundred court was included in the grant the sheriff was deprived of the profits of its pleas. He was therefore permitted to recoup himself in his account by charging the yearly rent blank; so that if that rent was £20, his farm was reduced by £20 clear. If on the other hand the hundred court was retained by the king, then his agent, the sheriff, charged the amount of the rent by tale, and thus reduced his farm not by £20 but by £19. The profits of the court were deemed to equal the difference between the two sums.

A different explanation of this passage has been given by the editors of the Dialogue,[1] who think

> that (*a*) the tenant paid an extra allowance for blanching at a fixed scale, (*b*) that he recouped himself from the profits of the hundred court when they were granted to him; otherwise the allowance was found by the sheriff from the same source.

But it seems to me that the tenant is not concerned in the matter at all. Many of these *terrae datae* had been alienated many years before, and they are entered year after year at the rental which they bore at the time of the grant. The sheriff has lost so much out of his farm, and he deducts a corresponding sum from the amount he pays in to the Treasury. If he has lost both the rent and the profits of the hundred court, he deducts the full amount of the rent; in other words he makes the allowance blank. If he has lost the rent

[1] Introduction, p. 33.

only, he makes the allowance *numero*, which meant an amount diminished by 5 per cent. In the former case the blanching is conventional or automatic ; no assay takes place ; just as we have seen the charge of £25 on the farm of Exeter represented on the roll as £25 12s. 6d.[1]

These four classes of allowances—alms, tithes, liveries, and lands granted—were made 'by the custom of the Exchequer' and did not need the authority of writs from the king.[2] All that was necessary was to compare the items with the entries in the preceding roll.[3] But when a grant of land was first made, the charter or writ for it had to be presented at the Michaelmas session of the Exchequer to authorize the allowance to the sheriff.[4] The changes in the other classes were usually of such small sums that we may take it that they were left to the sheriff's discretion. The sheriff had however to produce his quittances for every item to show that he had actually paid all the monies for which he claimed allowance.

The next class consists of sums expended from the farm by the king's writs, and its items are called 'casual' in distinction from the 'settled' disbursements. In each entry the king's writ had to be

---

[1] Above, p. 33.

[2] Dialogus i. 5 p. 186; ii. 6 p. 221.

[3] ii. 4 p. 220.

[4] If the grant was an advance (*praestitum*) or was made *quamdiu regi placuerit*, it did not pass at a man's death to his heirs: ibid., pp. 220 f.

expressly mentioned, and this fact introduced a difference in the procedure by which this whole class of allowances was accounted for. Hitherto it was the treasurer who examined the sheriff; but now the sheriff hands over the writs which he has received to the chancellor's clerk, and he reads them aloud and passes them on to the treasurer, so that he may dictate the form of entry in the roll.[1] In some cases, as in building works, it was not possible to state beforehand in the writ the precise amount of expenditure authorized. It therefore named two or three men who were to 'view' the work, and they had to appear at the Exchequer and certify upon oath that the sum charged by the sheriff was duly expended. Another writ, or precept, in which the sum was named, was then drawn up at the Exchequer under the witness of the president; and then the sheriff received his allowance.[2]

These payments by writ are from an historical point of view by far the most interesting on the roll. They give information about the king's movements, they tell us what guests arrived from abroad, they furnish evidence of the hospitality maintained at the Court and of the building works in progress, and even tell us particulars about dress and other personal matters. Specimens may be found under every county, but Hampshire and London and Middlesex supply perhaps the most abundant

[1] Dialogus ii. 6 p. 221. [2] ii. 8 p. 223.

materials of historical interest. I quote some extracts from a pipe of the latter county:

[1] For ten casks of wine sent to Nottingham against Christmas £10 by the king's writ. And for carriage of the same wine 40s. by the same writ. For three casks of French wine and two barrels of wine of Lorraine sent to Woodstock £6 14s. by the same writ. And for carting the same wine 4s. by the same writ. And for harness for the packhorse of the king's chapel 9s. by the king's writ. And for 100 ells of red scarlet and again for other 12 ells of red scarlet and for 12 ells of Persian scarlet and for 20 divers gowns and for 10 cloths of lawn [and other drapery] £92 14s. 5d. by the king's writ. . . . And to Alnoð the engineer 20 marks for repairing the king's chamber at Westminster by the king's writ and by view of Edward Blund and William Grand. . . . And for 3000 lb. of wax £43 9s. 7d. by [the king's] writ. And for the king's tent and for cloth and ropes for making the same tent £15 17s. 1d. by the same writ. . . . And in payments (*in soltis*) by the king's writ to certain Jews £73 3s. 3d. And to Roger Falistorp the falconer 20s. in advance upon his livery by the king's writ.

Besides these allowances for expenditure by writ, there were certain others which, though not so authorized, were admitted, like the alms and liveries which appear earlier on the roll, by the custom of the Exchequer. The principal charges under this head were those arising out of the administration of justice. First, there were the expenses of executing sentences (*iustitiae*) and conducting ordeals (*iudicia*).[2] Secondly, regular wages

[1] Roll of 23 Henry II, pp. 197 f.

[2] Dialogus ii. 6, 7 pp. 221 f.

of a penny a day and the cost of their transport were paid to approvers (*probatores*) who, to escape the full penalty of their crime, 'turned,' as we should say, 'king's evidence' or acted as champions in trial by battle.[1] The sheriff was also allowed to charge without writ for the conveyance of the king's treasure from place to place by order of the treasurer and chamberlains or of their servants.[2]

[3] Again, if a sturgeon, turbot, or whale, or any sea beast of this sort is caught, the sheriff supplies what is necessary for pickling and other requirements and is allowed without writ. Again, he can incur expenditure on the king's vines and their vintage,[4] and in supplying vessels and other necessaries on his oath without writ.

With these charges, whether with or without writ, the account of the *corpus comitatus*, or principal farm, is brought to a conclusion. Then

after a small space is put the account of the arrears *de veteri firma comitatus*, that is of any sums which chance to remain over from the previous year, supposing that the sheriff who was then in office was changed; but if the same sheriff continues in the present year he makes his discharge for the old farm before beginning his account for the new.[5]

Any entries which follow are those of distinct accounts, for instance of guilds, which were paid

---

1 ii. 7 p. 222.

2 Ibid., pp. 222 f.

3 Ibid., p. 223.

4 The king had a vineyard, for instance, in Huntingdonshire: Roll of 5 Henry II, p. 54.

5 See above, p. 155.

in full or balanced separately. In working out the account of a farm we have to begin by taking all the payments blank as net payments and all the others, whether specified as *numero* or not, as payments by tale. All the payments by tale have to be 'blanched' or diminished by a shilling in the pound, eight pence in the mark, and so in proportion, down to a penny in twenty pence. The simplest plan of reckoning the figures is to cast up the two classes of payments separately, and then to reduce the payments *numero* and add their sum to the total of the payments blank. When the whole amount is arrived at, we have to reckon in the sum paid into the Treasury and the debit balance, and the resulting figures give the amount of the farm. If the balance is a surplus, it must be deducted.

We must be careful however not to add up the figures mechanically, without noticing that there is an irregularity in the roll; for the model described in the Dialogue could not always, in the pressure of business, be exactly followed. I may give an example from the Gloucestershire account for the 22nd year of Henry II.[1] This first concludes with the words, 'And he owes £27 19s. 8d. and renders account for that debt.' Then it is remembered that only a half-year's rent had been entered for William Pinkney's lands at Slaughter and Cheltenham instead of that for a whole year.

---

[1] p. 123.

So a new entry is made : 'And in lands granted to William of Pinkeni by the king's writ £15 by tale,' that is £14 5s. blank. 'And he owes £13 14s. 8d. blank,' which is the difference between £27 19s. 8d. and £14 5s. Another caution may be added. It is very easy to misread the figures in the roll, not only because they are written in Roman numerals but also because they are often expressed in unfamiliar forms, as 'vi. li. xiid.',[1] or where an unusual denomination, such as a mark of gold, is mentioned. But if we read the rolls with care, it is extremely seldom that we shall find any error in their reckoning, though it must be confessed that many mistakes have been made by those who have attempted to expound their method.[2]

When the account of the sheriff's farm is ended, the second—usually by far the longer—part of

1 Thus in the Ramsey chartulary an extract from the Roll of 4 John is entered in which the words *c. et xiii. li. et x. d. et ob.* are miscopied as *de centum tredecim libris decem solidis obolo*. The editors have noted the variant but profess themselves unable to see that it explains the difference between the sum of the items as printed, £396 19s. 3d., and the correct total, £396 10s. 1d.: Chartularium Monasterii de Rameseia, i (1884) 227, and note 10.

2 For example, the explanation of the sheriff's account given with a specimen balance sheet of 5 Henry II in the Introduction to the Pipe Rolls, pp. 48–51, omits to blanch the *terrae datae* and erroneously excludes £30 at Trentham, with the result that the farm of Staffordshire appears as £112 7s. 11d. instead of £140.

the account begins. It differs from the earlier part in two respects. The entries under the farm were all expressed, as I have said, in terms of negatives, as deductions from a fixed sum. I have often spoken of them as charges or payments, for such in fact they were; but from the point of view of the account they were discharges or allowances. In the following part, on the contrary, all the sums mentioned are sums actually due from the sheriff to the Exchequer. Many of them were indeed reduced by payments by the king's writ, and in many cases the sheriff was not able to get in all the money for which he was responsible. But still it was all a matter of direct payment not of deduction from a fixed amount. It was probably a consequence of the fact that the payments had not to be deducted from a definite sum but were simply charged as they stood, that the entries under the following heads are by no means so regularly arranged as those of the 'principal account'. The titles of the subdivisions are often omitted, and entries often appear in unexpected places.

First, after a space of six or seven lines, there follows the farm of purprestures and encroachments, and of manors and woods from which a yearly rent was due and paid.[1]

[2] In the middle of the line is written in large letters the heading *De purpresturis et esceatis*, and at the beginning of the next, *The same sheriff renders account for the farm*

[1] Dialogus i. 5 p. 186. [2] ii. 10 p. 225.

of purprestures and escheats, to wit, for £10 from this man and for £20 from that, and so forth, according to the form entered from the roll of the itinerant justices in the roll of the year: *total £100.* Then at the end of the same line where the total is given, follows *In the Treasury £20 in so many tallies, and he owes four score pounds,* or *He has paid into the Treasury and is quit.*

The purprestures (or *propresturae* as they are called in the rolls) are encroachments by building or occupation upon royal lands by private persons, the value of which was assessed by the itinerant justices and the rent levied by the sheriff.[1] With them are included payments for assarts or clearings in the forest. The escheats, or profits of escheated lands, are in like manner grouped with other feudal incidents, wardships and reliefs. Sometimes other miscellaneous payments are found under this heading, such as arrears of scutage and charges for which a reference to other parts of the roll are added. It was a convenient place for entering various small items which formed neither part of the farm nor of the more considerable sections of the roll recorded later on. I should add that many of the rents received from escheats were charged with payments by the king's writ, and were diminished by *terrae datae,* so that their account has the appearance of a miniature sheriff's farm; but there is here no balance: the monies received are

[1] See the Tractatus de Legibus et Consuetudinibus Regni Angliae, attributed to Ranulf Glanvill, ix. 11 (ed. 1780) p. 150.

accounted for in full. The rents of woods and forests are a small item, entered as follows: *The same sheriff, or another named, renders account for £20 for the rent of such or such a wood or forest of Northamptonshire.*[1] Some of these rents were charged with tithes to cathedral churches; in Northamptonshire payable to Lincoln,[2] in Wiltshire and Hampshire to Salisbury.[3] All these entries are found mixed up with the purprestures and escheats, and are sometimes added after the farm without any special heading.[4] Among them appear the assessments of royal manors which were not included in the farm because they did not pass into the king's hands until a time subsequent to the settlement of the farm: such were King's Bromley and Newcastle in Staffordshire.

The second division of this part of the roll is perfunctorily dealt with in the first book of the Dialogue,[5] where it is simply said that 'after a space there is given an account of the debts for which the sheriff is summoned, with the names of the judges to whom they belong'. This indicates what is commonly a very long series of entries, most of them of small amount, specifying the profits arising from judicial proceedings. It also includes the whole series of taxes levied on land-

---

[1] Dialogus ii. 11 pp. 231 f.

[2] Thus in the Roll of 23 Henry II p. 88.

[3] Ibid., pp. 98, 167.

[4] Thus under Worcestershire, ibid., p. 64.

[5] i. 5 p. 187.

holders under the names of Danegeld, scutage, *donum*, aid, and tallage.[1] Bishop Richard tells us something of these latter payments in a different connexion, but says not a word of them in his description of the roll. Perhaps he was justified, for the proceeds of these great sources of revenue, or so much of them as the sheriff could collect, were paid in as they were received, and were therefore of little interest from the point of view of the form of the account, all the less because the order in which they were recorded was extremely capricious.

The judicial profits are entitled *placita et conventiones*, pleas and covenants or agreements. We should call them alike 'fines'; but the distinction is between payments which are compulsory and those which are optional (*oblata spontanea*).[2] If a man is convicted by the king's court, whether *coram rege* or before the justices itinerant, he is at the king's mercy and can only escape by payment of a prescribed sum of money, an 'amercement'. If on the other hand he wishes to obtain seisin of land claimed by him, he sues for it and when successful pays a 'fine', because it is the end of the litigation. These payments were distinguished as *oblata in rem* and *oblata in spem*.[3] The former are those in which a man offers

---

[1] Scutage, the murder fine, and Danegeld are discussed, in connexion with the exemption of the officers of the Exchequer, in i. 9–11 pp. 201–204.

[2] ii. 12 p. 232.

[3] See for what follows ii. 23 pp. 242 f.

a sum of money, and the king accepts it, for obtaining a franchise or estate, or the wardship of a minor, or anything else which enures to his advantage or honour. The latter are offered for access to the king's court or for hastening proceedings at law, not (bishop Richard is careful to explain) for securing a favourable sentence. The money is not paid until the suit is determined. If the suitor neglects to proceed, he is still required to pay, though the king may abate the amount. If his action fails, he pays nothing. For every fine levied the queen received 'her gold' (*aurum reginae*), a tax of a mark of gold, or six pounds, on every hundred marks of silver, that is to say, of 9 per cent., and her clerk attended at the Exchequer to claim the payment.[1] The section of the roll headed *Nova placita et novae conventiones* contains the sums charged at the eyre of the itinerant justices during the current year. Sometimes the justices are named; sometimes, when they are not called 'new', the pleas are of a preceding eyre.[2]

---

[1] Dialogus ii. 26 p. 244. In the seventeenth century it was sought to revive the claim of the queen consort. Besides the treatise by Hakewill mentioned above, p. 16 note (see the Calendar of State Papers, Domestic Series, 1603–1610, p. 383), William Prynne in 1668 dedicated to queen Katherine his Aurum Reginae or a compendious Tractate and chronological Collection of Records in the Tower and Court of Exchequer concerning Queen-Gold.

[2] See bishop Stubbs's preface to the Gesta Henrici, ii. p. lxiii note 2.

The returns were taken from the justices' rolls and, like the later items in the sheriff's farm, were checked not by the treasurer but by the chancellor's clerk. The amercements for the forest usually form a separate heading and amount to a considerable sum. A short entry 'from those who have paid in full' (*de his qui totum reddiderunt*) is a compendious statement of arrears paid in, commonly of small amounts, with a reference for the particulars to the roll of the preceding year; but payments belonging to the current year are often added under the same heading. The payment of fines was as a rule spread over more than one year.

The difference of the principle on which Danegeld and scutage and aid were assessed and the arbitrary nature of the *donum* and tallage do not affect the account: the sheriff has only to state the sums due and the sums collected. What interests the Exchequer is to be sure that the deductions made from them were correct. For not only were many persons relieved from Danegeld, scutage, and the murder fine, and their quittance had to be recorded; but also a part or the whole of a number of fines and amercements was forgiven by the king, and the writ authorizing the discharge had to be produced.

Finally there is a heading 'Of the chattels of fugitives and persons mutilated' (*De catallis fugitivorum et mutilatorum*), under which are entered the proceeds of the sale of the effects of criminals.[1] These are paid in in full.

Outside the sheriff's account, though included in the same roll, are the accounts of the cities, boroughs, and honours which accounted separately. They were only a limited number: the Dialogue mentions as examples Lincoln, Winchester, Meon, Berkhampsted, and Colchester;[2] in all there were about fourteen boroughs[3] and a varying number of honours which so accounted. London of course stood on a special footing, since from near the end of Henry I's reign its citizens held the county of Middlesex at a farm, and thenceforward London and Middlesex constituted an indivisible unit.[4] These accounts of boroughs and honours were drawn up exactly like farms of counties on a smaller scale, with their alms and liveries, *terrae datae* and allowances; and they were balanced separately. Each may be followed by entries of amercements and fines, aids and scutage. The normal position of these independent accounts was at the end of the counties to which they belonged; but there are many exceptions to this rule.

---

[1] Dialogus i. 5 p. 187.

[2] i. 5 p. 186.

[3] Dr. Parow, pp. 29 f., reckons 42; but he includes a number of farms which do not appear under distinct headings on the roll and which were probably paid through the sheriff.

[4] See Round, Geoffrey de Mandeville, pp. 343–373; and compare The Commune of London, pp. 229–235.

When the account of a particular sheriff has been adjusted, then at length a balance is struck with the farm as recorded on the tax roll.

[1] First, the calculator distributes counters in the proper spaces corresponding to the farm paid in at the current term. Then the sum which has been tested is blanched by the amount of the 'combustion' [or loss by the assay], a little tally with a note of that amount is attached to the tally [of the unblanched sum], and the remainder is recorded upon it. In like manner what was paid and blanched at Easter is recorded on the same tally. The two 'combustions' are combined upon it. Then the treasurer brings forth the tax roll (*rotulus exactorius*) and causes the amount of the farm to be shown by counters on the board on the side nearest him. Below this sum is first deducted the sum paid into the Treasury and blanched; secondly the lands granted by the king blank; thirdly the payments by the king's writ or otherwise, each of these last being blanched by a deduction of 12d. in the pound.

The sum was done simply by removing the counters in pairs from the upper and the lower rows. If nothing was left the sheriff was declared quit, *Et quietus est*; if there was anything remaining in the upper row of counters, the sum was entered in a fresh line on the roll, with the words *Et debet* so much. Then at last the figures indicating the amount paid into the Treasury were inserted at the head of the roll. It was left to the end in order to avoid the risk of having to make erasures, 'which should be specially avoided in numbers and names and causes.'

[1] Dialogus ii. 27 p. 246.

VIII

THE EXCHEQUER AND THE KING'S COURT

In the two earliest examples that have been found of the use of the word Exchequer its barons appear as officers of the law. In one they are to constrain a sheriff to make a payment out of his farm:[1] in the other the bishop of London is commanded to do full right to the abbot of Westminster as touching the men who broke into a church of his by arms at night; otherwise the barons of the Exchequer should cause it to be done that the king might hear no complaint of it for default of right.[2] One might infer from these instances that there existed a Court of Exchequer which had cognizance both of civil and criminal pleas. But this inference would be premature: there is no mention yet of a Court. As soon as the Court is named, it is 'the king's Court at the Exchequer', just as a few years before the Exchequer was established a suit was heard 'in the king's Court in the Treasury'.[3]

---

[1] Above, p. 39. The writ is addressed *Rogero episcopo Saresberiae et baronibus scaccarii*, and the order is *ut ita constringatis vicecomitem ut eas* [*xxv libras*] *reddat eis* [*canonicis S. Trinitatis Londoniae*], *sicut faceretis de mea propria firma*: Madox ix. 2 p. 188 *r*.

[2] Above, p. 39.

[3] Above, p. 34 note 2.

The pleas which were held first in the Treasury and then at the Exchequer were alike held in the king's Court. What is the meaning of the combination, 'in the king's Court at the Exchequer'?

We know that proceedings in the royal palace, wherever the king might be, were conducted in the king's Court, whether they were heard by the king in person or by his justiciar. But the pleas heard before the justices itinerant were equally pleas in the king's Court.[1] 'We are tempted,' says Maitland,[2] 'to use terms which are more precise than those that were current in the twelfth century. In particular we are wont to speak of *the* Curia Regis without remembering that the definite article is not in our documents. Any court held in the king's name by his delegates is Curia Regis.' The distinction is that of the sort of justice administered: it is the king's justice, as contrasted with that of the local courts of the hundred and shire or the feudal courts of the manor and franchise. This justice was not to be

---

[1] Mr. Round gives reasons for believing that, at the earliest time for which fines (that is, final concords) are preserved, a distinction was made between fines levied 'in the king's Court before the justices' and those 'before the justices' when the king was absent; but the distinction was not long preserved, and though the levy is not stated to have been made in the king's Court in the latter cases, the precedent plea is so stated: see Feudal England, pp. 509–515; and The earliest Fines, in the English Historical Review, xii (1897) 293–302.

[2] History of English Law, i. 132.

had for nothing. It was necessary to obtain a writ and to pay a fine. The advantages of a hearing before a more competent and experienced body of judges than could be found in the local courts was not at once appreciated. So far as our information goes, in the earlier time the king's Court, except so far as it held the pleas of the crown, only gradually developed from a Court for tenants in chief to a Court to which recourse could be taken 'for default of justice' in the lower courts; but by degrees it acquired popularity and the number of suits brought before it became very large.

Now the king had no public buildings which were definitely set apart for legal proceedings. He had his Hall in the palace of Westminster, where he or his justiciar heard causes *coram rege*; and near by there was the Exchequer which was only used for its special purposes for two short periods in the year. Moreover, there existed no professional body of judges. The justiciar, the *capitalis iustitia* as he is called in the Dialogue, was no more a professional judge than are the lords justices who to this day are appointed in Ireland during the absence of the lord lieutenant: he was the king's vicegerent. Now in the Exchequer there was to be found a staff of men, by origin members of the Household, who were habitually accustomed to decide questions connected with the revenue. When, as was constantly the case, they recorded fines paid for the settlement of rights to land and such matters, the record indicated the result of a process of legal inquiry. It may be said that the 'higher business', the *scientia*,[1] of the Exchequer was throughout judicial. With this, the only available, staff at hand, it was natural that the king should look to it for the consideration of suits which mostly arose over questions of property and possession. The pleas of the crown, criminal justice, he reserved in theory for his own hearing: those which concerned the rights of his subjects he handed over to the Exchequer; and when he dealt with them throughout the country by means of itinerant justices, the justices he employed were not only sheriffs, great churchmen, and other county magnates, but also—sometimes the majority or all of them[2]—were men who acted at the Exchequer board. If this view is correct, it will follow that, when we read that a cause was heard 'in the king's Court at the Exchequer', the words 'at the Exchequer' indicate merely that it was heard at a certain place and before the barons;[3] it will not exclude the fact that the barons might equally be called upon to hold pleas *coram rege* elsewhere.

---

[1] See above, p. 103.

[2] See below, p. 179 and note 2.

[3] This is the opinion of Edward Foss, The Judges of England, ii (1848) 167; cf. i. 178 f.

An interesting passage in the Dialogue[1] tells us of a *thalamus secretorum*,[2] a privy chamber, situate hard by the house where the Exchequer was.

> Hither the barons repair when a doubtful point is laid before them at the Exchequer, concerning which they prefer to treat apart rather than in the ears of all, but especially that they may not hinder the accounts which are being rendered: so, while they are occupied in their counsels, the accustomed course of the account proceeds; but if any new question arises, it is referred to them.

It is possible that this was the king's privy chamber in the palace, for in the roll of the seventh year of Richard I there is a payment

> [3] for two cloths bought for the Exchequer of the barons in the king's *thalamus* and for another Exchequer *in solio*,

where *solium* I take to mean an upper chamber.[4] It is tempting to see here the Court of Exchequer, a Court for revenue cases, fully established. But it would be dangerous to speak, as Foss seems to do,[5] of that Court as already 'a constituent part

---

[1] i. 7 pp. 195 f.

[2] Madox, iv. 9 p. 130 *b, c*, quotes instances from the rolls of 8 Richard I and later of payments for the furniture of the *thalamus baronum*.

[3] Quoted by Madox, p. 130*d*.

[4] There is evidence in Ducange for the use of *solium* as equivalent to *solarium*. Madox's explanation 'the Throne-like Exchequer (perhaps because it was framed like a Throne or Court)' seems wanting in probability. Foss, i. 180, thinks that a throne was set there.

[5] The Judges of England, ii. 167.

of the Curia Regis, but still a distinct branch, confined to the revenue'. I would rather put it in this way. The barons of the Exchequer were invested with judicial power primarily over disputed matters which arose out of claims and counter-claims relating to the king's revenue. Their experience in such matters led naturally to their being employed in the hearing of suits between subjects, of common pleas; but neither did this create a Court of Common Pleas, for such pleas might be held elsewhere than in the Exchequer.

In 1178 indeed Henry II may have designed to place them under separate judicature. The author of the Gesta Regis Henrici tells us, in a well-known passage, that

> [1] the king made enquiry as touching the justices whom he had appointed in England, whether they treated the men of the kingdom well and with moderation; and when he learned that the land and the people of the land were greatly burthened by so great a multitude of justices, for they were in number eighteen,[2] he by the counsel of the wise men of his realm chose five only, namely two clerks and three laymen, and they were all of his private Household. And he ordained that these five should hear all complaints of the kingdom, and do right; and that they should not depart from the king's Court, but should remain there to hear the complaints of the people; so

[1] i. 207 f.

[2] 'All the eighteen justices of 1176 were officers of the Exchequer:' Stubbs, Constitutional History of England, § 163.

that if any question arose among them which they could not bring to a termination, it should be presented to the king and determined as might seem good to him and to the wise men of the realm.

This statement has been taken by bishop Stubbs [1] and by Mr. Melville Bigelow [2] to describe the origination of the Court of king's Bench; but the words mentioning the suits to be heard point rather to common pleas. Moreover, a different arrangement was made in the next year, and the six judges then appointed were also sent out on eyre in the northern counties. Neither expedient seems to have been of permanent importance.

Meanwhile there is abundant evidence of common law suits being heard at the Exchequer. For instance, when, towards the end of Henry II's reign, the king entrusted the abbacy of Abingdon during a vacancy to one of his clerks, this guardian seized not only the possessions belonging to the abbot's 'chamber' but also the estates of the monastery into the king's hand. The prior therefore brought the matter before the justiciar Ranulf Glanvill and claimed that the rights of the monastery were protected by charter. He went to the justiciar at the Exchequer, and Glanvill took counsel 'with the bishops and other justices who sat with him at the Exchequer', and gave judgement in favour of the

[1] Preface to the Gesta Henrici, i. pp. lxxi, lxxiv f.; Constitutional History of England, § 233.

[2] History of Procedure, p. 89.

monks.[1] This was manifestly not a meeting of the board of Exchequer, but of the king's Court sitting there.

A class of suit which was very commonly heard before the barons of the Exchequer was that which led to a final concord or fine of land. When it first appears it was already a collusive suit between two parties, one of whom desired to sell and the other to buy; there was a simulated conflict and a final concord settled by a payment of money and the drawing up of a chirograph or indenture in two parts, recording the transaction. This deed was brought before the Court and sealed. The advantage of this procedure was that it secured the evidence of the record and that the authority of the Court protected the demandant.[2] It can be traced in principle to a much earlier time; and the form which became regular emerges in 1170.[3] In this example there is a slight variation of phrase (*concordia* simply, instead of *finalis concordia*), but otherwise the type is already established. From 1175 a series of final concords is preserved:[4] some are made before the justices

---

1 Chronicon Monasterii de Abingdon, ii. 297 f.

2 Pollock and Maitland, History of English Law, ii. 94 ff.

3 Chartae antiquae DD. 31, printed by Mr. Round, The earliest Fines, in the English Historical Review, xii. 300 f.

4 See Round, ubi supra, pp. 293–300, and Feudal England, pp. 509–516; Maitland, introduction to Select Pleas of the Crown, i (1888) pp. xxvii, xxviii.

itinerant, but when the suit was held at Westminster, it was frequently at the Exchequer. The record is sometimes entered at length on the pipe roll, even when the fine is not said to have been made at the Exchequer.[1] In 1195 it was ordered that the indenture should be tripartite, and that the third part should be preserved as a record in the Treasury. This was called the *pes finis*, the foot of the fine, where it is suggested that there is a confusion between the Latin *pes* and the Old French *pes*, meaning peace or concord. The feet of fines preserved from that date form an important body of evidence for the history of the conveyance of lands.[2]

Many other common pleas continued to be held at the Exchequer, and it is not until the reign of John that the justices *in banco*, the justices of the common Bench or, as they were called later, of common pleas, definitely make their appearance.[3] Whether any sharp distinction was yet made between this body of judges who held these pleas and those who heard cases *coram rege*, the future judges of the king's Bench, is a difficult question, and one which does not concern our present

[1] The earliest instance appears to be a chirograph of 1 December 1182, which is entered on the Roll of the preceding Michaelmas, 28 Henry II pp. 107 f.

[2] The Feet of Fines of 7 and 8 Richard I were issued by the Pipe Roll Society in 1896.

[3] See Maitland's argument in the introduction to Select Pleas of the Crown, i. pp. xiii–xix. Foss, ii. 165–173, was of a different opinion.

purpose. All that we are interested to show is that a separation of Courts was not an essential element in the development. When the Great Charter made a famous enactment about common pleas, it said nothing about a distinct Court: it ordered simply that they should not follow the king's Court but should be held in a certain fixed place.[1] For many years afterwards it is impossible to separate the judges who held common pleas from those who held pleas *coram rege*;[2] and it may be doubted whether even as late as 1258 the king's Bench can be considered to have been definitively constituted.[3] So too we have to wait until 1234 before we find persons formally appointed to be barons of the Exchequer,[4] until 1236 before the plea-rolls of the Court begin,[5] and until 1317 before the existing treasurer, Walter of Norwich, is created in reward of his long services

---

1 Article 17. In exactly the same way William I enacted that *nullus episcopus vel archidiaconus de legibus episcopalibus amplius in hundret placita teneant* (Liebermann, Gesetze der Angelsachsen, i. 485). He did not, as has been supposed, thereby establish a new Court; he merely forbade that certain pleas should be held in the hundred court.

2 See Foss, ii. 174–186.

3 See the writ of 3 October 1258 described in the Calendar of Patent Rolls, Henry III, 1247–1258, p. 652; 1908.

4 Close Rolls, Henry III, 1231–1234, pp. 569 f., 1905.

5 There is one roll of Henry III's 20th–21st year, and there are two of the 43rd to the 45th year; but the regular series begins in the 51st year: Lists and Indexes, Public Record Office, iv, ed. 1910, p. 66.

chief baron of the Exchequer.[1] The Court of Exchequer did not acquire jurisdiction in equity until Tudor times. In like manner there is no need to speak in this place of the Court of Chancery, for that Court has not yet come into existence.[2]

But it will not be amiss to say something of the Chancery as an office of administration, because not merely was its business closely connected at many points with that of the Exchequer but there is reason to believe that that business was carried on in the same building. We are so much accustomed to the separation of public offices, when every office has a distinct building and all the higher officials have rooms to themselves, that it is difficult to imagine the whole machinery of government being carried on in one place. Yet until recent times it was common in our great public schools for several classes or forms to receive their several instruction in a single room. And so it was with the administration staff of the early Plantagenet kings. The Chancery, the body of clerks under the chancellor who did the king's secretarial business, sat in the Exchequer; and the arrangement was the easier, since the Exchequer only sat for a limited time at two periods of the

1 Madox xxi. 3 p. 585 g.

2 Of course the chancellor might be and was employed on judicial business, but he acted by the king's commission as a member of the Court, not because he was chancellor.

year, and when it sat required clerks from the Chancery to check and 'control' the accounts.[1]

That the head of this office, the chancellor, was not a dignitary of the highest rank may be argued from the fact that no bishop was appointed chancellor until after the death of Henry II.[2] All this time when a chancellor was made a bishop he ceased to be chancellor either at once or very soon afterwards.[3] But the office was growing in importance, and under Richard I its tenure by a bishop was admitted. William of Longchamp became chancellor on the king's accession, in less than a fortnight he was elected bishop of Ely, and soon afterwards was made justiciar as well. In October 1191 he was ejected from the justiciarship and left England; but he retained the title of chancellor until his death in 1197. He was succeeded as chancellor by Eustace, who followed him also as bishop of Ely. These two officers mark the time of transition, when a chancellor might retain the king's seal after promotion to

---

[1] See above, pp. 113 ff.

[2] Henry's son Geoffrey was, it is true, elect of Lincoln when he was made chancellor in 1181; but he was required to resign the see. For this resignation, however, there were other reasons, and too much stress should not be laid upon it.

[3] Henry I's chancellor Geoffrey, who was consecrated bishop of Durham in August 1133, seems to have continued chancellor until the end of the reign. But all this time the king was abroad, and may have been unwilling to make a change.

a bishopric. Next after them came the first prelate who was appointed chancellor, no less a man than Hubert Walter, archbishop of Canterbury, who was given the seal at the accession of John and kept it until his death in July 1205.

When the Chancery was removed into a building of its own has not been definitely ascertained. Madox thought that the change took place in the course of Richard I's reign, but he put forward his opinion only as a conjecture.

> [1] It appears that when K. Richard was in foreign parts, William de Longchamp the king's chief justicier and chancellour was put out of his office of chief justicier by the power and intrigue of John earl of Moreton. After which, although he continued chancellour for some short time, it is likely he did not attend and act at the Exchequer as before. By which means, the business of the Chancery which used to be done at the Exchequer might, probably, be done in another place, or might be put into a new method. In which new or separate method it might afterwards continue; as in truth it hath ever since continued, in this particular. I cannot say, that the separation of the Chancery from the Exchequer was brought about purely by the means or in the manner here mentioned. However, it is, I suppose, a happy thing in the event: because thereby the publick have gained many bundles of Chancery-rolls, which are very historical and instructive.

Since, however, William Longchamp left England immediately after his removal from the justiciarship in 1191 and never came back to England, he cannot have been directly responsible for any

---

[1] iv. 10 p. 132.

changes in the official machinery which were made after that date.

I am disposed rather to trace the reorganization of business and of offices which marks the reigns of Richard I and John to the activity of Hubert Walter. He, more than any man of his time, united within himself experience in every branch of the administration. He had served as a baron of the Exchequer as early as 1184; he had kept Henry II's seal when he was abroad in 1189; [1] on his return from the crusade he was justiciar during years when finance was the most pressing call upon his energies; and he was finally chancellor. The nephew of the great justiciar Ranulf Glanvill, it has been suggested that he was in fact the author of the treatise on the Laws and Customs of the Kingdom which has passed for seven hundred years as the work of his uncle.[2] Though it may be true that the practice of enrolling the pleas of the king's Court was adopted from the Exchequer before his time,[3] yet the regular series of rolls begins in 1194 soon after he was made justiciar.[4] His knowledge of the

---

1 Epistolae Cantuarienses, ed. Stubbs, 1865, pp. 282 f., 284.

2 Pollock and Maitland, History of English Law, i. 143.

3 See above, p. 117.

4 The establishment of the Exchequer of the Jewry as a separate but subordinate office of account also belongs to about this time, between 1194 and 1198: see Charles Gross, The Exchequer of the Jews of England, in Papers read at the Anglo-Jewish

business of government in all its branches, financial, judicial, and administrative, would naturally suggest to him the convenience of making the secretary's office, the Chancery, a separate department. Now on the coronation of John on 27 May 1199 Hubert was appointed chancellor, and three weeks later we find the system already established of enrolling the charters and writs of the Chancery, on a method analogous to the enrolments of the king's Court and of the Exchequer, which continued unchanged in principle down to modern times.[1] The introduction of this system does not of course necessarily coincide with the setting up of a department locally distinct from the other offices of government. But it appears more reasonable to assign this change to a time of regular organization than to a date like that when William Longchamp fled from England and left the Chancery, so far as we can see, without any directing officer.

The withdrawal of the chancellor from the Exchequer was not only, as is well known, of decisive importance for the history of the

Historical Exhibition, 1887, i. 174, 1888.

[1] The charter rolls themselves are not preserved before July 1199; but there exists among the Miscellaneous Records of the Exchequer (King's Remembrancer) an enrolment of seven charters dated on 17 and 18 June. This is printed by sir Thomas Duffus Hardy in the introduction to the Rotuli Chartarum, p. xl.

Chancery;[1] it also led to a remarkable shifting of the centre of gravity at the Exchequer. That board had been constituted on the principle that the king should have control of the financial administration by means of his own secretary, the chancellor, assisted by his clerk and writer. Now the chancellor was gone, and his clerk, so far from being a representative of the Chancery, became one of the chief officers of the Exchequer, and in course of time, as chancellor of the Exchequer, its virtual head. The writer of the chancellor's roll was designed to act as a check upon the writer of the great roll; but the two officials became colleagues in the Pipe Office. The control of the Exchequer by the Chancery ceased to exist. Its place was taken by the two remembrancers, in origin confidential servants whom the king deputed to watch the accounts: they became instead officers of the Exchequer, and, so far as the work of detail and routine was concerned, they executed most of the duties which had once belonged to the treasurer. As the treasurer ceased more and more to act in matters of finance, the chancellor of the Exchequer rose to a position of still greater power, but it was in policy and chief supervision rather than in routine that his authority was exerted.

The treasurer's clerk, whose business was

---

1 See sir W. R. Anson, The Law and Custom of the Constitution, ii. part ii. 255.

confined to the Receipt, became the under-treasurer, and his post was usually held by the chancellor of the Exchequer, who thus secured practical supremacy in both departments. The external control too of the Treasury of Receipt, which had once intermittently existed, was given up. In the twelfth century the king had entrusted its audit to men of high rank in his Court:[1] by the beginning of the fourteenth the duty was left to an official of the Treasury, the tally-writer,[2] who in course of time acquired the title of auditor of the Receipt of the Exchequer.[3] A new system of external audit had to be created in modern times.[4] Perhaps the last link which had connected the Exchequer with the king's Court was destroyed when the duty of the marshal to take oaths from accountants was handed over to the cursitor baron of the Exchequer.

---

[1] *Cum a rege vel mandato regis a magnis regni compotus a thesaurario et camerariis regni totius receptae suscipitur*: Dialogus i. 5 p. 183; cf. i. 1 p. 172. It was for this reason that the writs of Liberate and the tallies of combustion were preserved: ibid., i. 6 pp. 188, 192. See Round, The Commune of London, pp. 77 ff.

[2] Madox xxiv. 11 pp. 737 f I do not here speak of the auditors of foreign accounts or of imprests because they belong to the internal reorganization of the Exchequer which lies outside my subject.

[3] In 1527, according to W. H. Black, appendix ii to the 4th Report of the Deputy-Keeper of the Public Records, 1843, p. 179.

[4] Compare above, pp. 9 f.

INDEX